PARALLELS
from the ORIGIN

Amyn Dahya

Vancouver, Canada

Copyright © 1999 Amyn Dahya

All rights reserved. No part of this publication may be reproduced without express written permission of the publisher, except in the case of brief quotations embodied in critical articles or reviews.

Canadian Cataloguing in Publication Data
Dahya, Amyn, 1957–
Parables from the origin

ISBN 0-9682683-2-3
1. Spiritual life. 2. Inspiration. I. Title.
BL624.D333 1999   291.4   C99-900582-0

Production: Reflections Publishing
Copy Editor: Neall Calvert
Text Design: Fiona Raven; Westpoint Graphics
Cover Design: Miles Christensen
Cover Painting: *Identity*, John Pitre

First printing May 1999

10 9 8 7 6 5 4 3 2 1

REFLECTIONS PUBLISHING
3908 Creekside Place
Burnaby, B.C. V5G 2P9
email: reflect@compuserve.com

Printed in Canada

DEDICATION

The Origin is Light
Light brings Life
Life brings Experience
Experience brings Knowledge
Knowledge brings Light.

*Such is the Cycle of Life
to which this book is dedicated.*

Table of Contents

	Dedication	*iii*
	Acknowledgments	*vi*
	Message to the Reader	*viii*
1	The Power of Love: The Parable of Ariana & Swaleem	1
2	The Saint in Central Park: The Parable of the Chief Executive	16
3	Making Wise Decisions: The Parable of the Gold Trader	23
4	The Alps: A Symbol of Humility	34
5	Fear: The Parable of the Slave	39
6	Detachment: The Parable of the Swiss Merchant	51
7	The Raindrop and the Blade of Grass: A Parable of Life Cycles	59
8	The Message of Reincarnation: The Parable of Tara	64
9	Kilimanjaro: A Parable of Life's Perspectives	73
10	The Ancient Church Bell: A Message from the Great Soul	82
11	Fences: The Parable of the Thai Farmer	88

12	The Eternal Pool: The Parable of Ebrahim and Sarah	94
13	The Instruments of Life: A Parable of Real People	101
14	The Bedouin: A Parable of the Desert	111
15	The Spinning Globe: A Parable of the Cycle of Life	118
16	Drawing Upon the Powers of Nature: The Parable of the Himalayan Shepherd	127
17	The Lighthouse: A Unique Experience in Meditation	138
18	Kaseem's Escape: The Parable of the Hermit	145
19	Kaseem's Escape: The Journey Home	154
20	Influencing Tomorrow: The Message of Self Empowerment	161
	Quotes for Reflection	170
	About the Author	185

Acknowledgments

A friend of mine once said, "A book has a life of its own." *Parables from the Origin* has been brought to life by the efforts of some very special people, whose contributions I wish to acknowledge with gratitude.

I would like to start by paying a special tribute to my wife, Karima, who has managed every aspect of publishing this book. Words could never acknowledge her contribution, because apart from her tireless efforts, she has always been there for me, as a pillar of strength in my life.

The love, support and understanding of our children—Adil, Aly, Raheena and Noorin—have also been a constant source of happiness and encouragement through all the fortunate and trying moments of my life.

I would also like to express my deepest gratitude to my father, Sadru, mother Nabat, brother Hanif and all members of my family, whose care and affection have formed the backbone of my life.

I wish to thank my adopted daughter Zahra, her husband Firdosh and my cousin Al-Karim for their assistance with the initial compilation of this book; and my dear friend Al-Karim Haji for his review of the manuscript.

I wish to pay tribute to my dear friend John Pitre, who has produced the magnificent artwork for the cover. John is truly an inspired artist and it is fitting that his work be used to convey the very first impression of *Parables from the Origin*.

I extend my sincere appreciation to all members of the Reflections Publishing team, whose dedication and efforts have led to the timely production of this book.

*M*essage to the *R*eader

In our daily lives, we go about performing our duties and responsibilities without thinking much about why we are here or what we are doing in this world. We accept each day as it comes and take in the experiences that we receive. These experiences leave an imprint in our lives and contribute towards shaping our attitudes towards everything around us. We generally assume that tomorrow will come and we plan and live our lives accordingly. I cannot say that this simple perspective is true for all people. However, it certainly represented how I looked at life until 1986, when I was involved in a near-fatal motorcycle accident in the heart of the Himalayan mountains.

I was riding in the evening along the main Kashmir highway to Srinagar. All of a sudden the front mudguard of the bike came loose and slid into the front wheel, causing the bike to catapult into the air at 80 kilometres per hour! For a split second, as I found myself flying in the air at a deadly speed, I felt as if my life was over! Then something very strange happened. I found myself being gently "placed" on the side of the road as I watched the bike burst into flames in the distance. Before the accident I had been wearing a woollen ski hat. After my "gentle" landing I was still wearing the hat! It was incredible that despite being violently hurled into the air, my head never touched the ground once as I landed! I escaped this horrific accident with minor injuries, to the amazement of my doctors.

After this accident I began to feel differently about myself and about everything around me. My inner self no longer felt the same. I used to be a very short-tempered and aggressive person. I now found myself transformed into a calm, tranquil personality. I was at peace with myself and my surroundings—an experience I had never known before. My wife, Karima, immediately noticed the change in me when I returned to Canada. Over the following months we talked a great deal about this change, because it was so dramatic. I definitely wasn't the man she had married four years previously!

Seven years later, in 1993, I once again began to experience a unique change in myself.

I found myself inspired with wonderful thoughts about life, its purpose, the Creator, the principles of Creation and lots more. I found myself waking up in the middle of the night and writing feverishly, without knowing what I was actually writing! At first I did not know what to do or how to react to these experiences. Each time I read what I had written, I was dumbfounded with the depth and simplicity of the knowledge that had flowed through me. I now understood the meaning of the phrase, "the Truth is always Simple." The other thing that amazed me was that the Old English vocabulary and the writing style that was reflected in my inspired works was markedly different to my normal style.

I shared these writings with my wife and close members of my family as, by and large, I considered them to be a private matter. I knew that these inspired words were coming from the Origin, the Source of Everything, and I was truly humbled by this whole experience. With time, as the inspirations grew more intense, I became aware that the knowledge I was receiving was not only for my own benefit. It had to be shared with humanity at large. In this process, my role was simply to be one of a postman delivering a letter!

In 1998 we released *Reflections from the Origin*, which was the first book carrying these inspired writings. This book dealt with subjects that encompassed all aspects of living, both from a material and a spiritual perspective. Clearly, all the knowledge that had been received could not be accommodated in one book—or even two books, for that matter. *Parables from the Origin*, which is comprised primarily of fables and stories, represents a continuation of the process of sharing in these inspired writings.

The feedback that I received on *Reflections from the Origin* included responses from people who said that they had found answers in certain chapters to burning questions they had carried within them for years. Some people also discovered a special personal bond with specific messages in the book, which served to enrich their lives, attitudes and outlooks.

While reading *Parables from the Origin*, take a few moments at the end of each parable to reflect upon its messages. It would also be rewarding to read each parable more than once, at different times, because new meanings may be discovered each time.

Since the stories are simple, they can be shared with children and people of all ages. Our ten-year-old daughter, Noorin, performed a play at school based on Chapter 1, "The Parable of Ariana and Swaleem", which portrays the power of love between a prince and a princess who lived many thousands of years ago! The response from her teachers and classmates was heartwarming, to say the least. Children have the tendency to identify dimensions surrounding events in a very innocent, yet deep, manner. We cannot deny that it is possible for our children to possess greater wisdom than we do!

In *Parables from the Origin* we have introduced "the Herald", who is an abstract character that receives the inspirations from the Origin and conveys them to the reader. Since the Herald has no recognizable human face, the reader can enjoy the process of being the sole participant in these communications with the Origin.

In conclusion, it is my hope and prayer that each of you may find special meanings and inspirations in this book. Writing it has certainly enriched my life.

ONE

THE *P*OWER OF *L*OVE:
THE PARABLE OF ARIANA & SWALEEM

The Voice of Inspiration asked the Herald: *"When you look at the Ocean at the time of sunset, what do you see?"*

He replied, "I see tranquillity and calmness. There is a special feeling that tells me that the Ocean is submitting to the will of the Sun at this time."

The Voice of Inspiration then said, *"That is true, for it is a spectacle of Humility that is revealed to humanity each day. Around you, there are symbols of Humility that must be recognized at all times. The Ocean is so vast and powerful. Yet it bows to the Sun when the day ends. It plays with the moon as the night passes. At Sunrise it is invigorated, and during the day the colours of the Ocean dominate the scenery in everything that surrounds it."*

The Voice of Inspiration continued: *"It is true that whatever dominates the scenery of the day always submits to a Greater Symbol at the end of the day. Such is the life of prominent people. Such is the life of ordinary people, plants, birds, animals and trees. Then, don't you often wonder how pride and vanity find their way into the hearts and minds of people, who are intelligent enough to know that above them is a Greater Symbol, of which they are also a part? Write about the story of Ariana and Swaleem, which conveys a clear understanding of Humility, humanity and the Greater Symbol."*

The Herald relates this true story of two very special people who lived well before the start of the Anno Domini (A.D.) calendar. The experiences of their lives teach some profound lessons that have been etched into the library of the Universe.

There was an ancient city that stood where three rivers meet. The rivers came from the North, the East and the West. The city was protected by strong walls of granite that had been built by the slaves of the Great King Saffiris. The city was called Tiberra, a name that comes from the powers of the three rivers. Saffiris ruled over the kingdom with great discipline. He was just and fair, yet he was firm and strong. He had a beautiful daughter, Ariana, who was his favourite child. Indeed Ariana was an extension of the great king's very own Soul.

One day the beautiful princess Ariana was taking a leisurely boat ride in the river with her friends. The sun shone brightly in the sky and the waters of the river carried the boat gently down their course. Suddenly, dark clouds began to gather in the sky. Before anyone had the time to turn the boats around and go back towards the city, a thunderstorm began to rage. Bolts of lightning shot from the sky, hitting trees that stood along the river bank and setting them aflame as if they were helpless twigs. The forces of the river began to change. The water began to flow with great power in the direction away from the city. As the boat began to speed down a course which had now become deadly, Ariana tried hard, along with her friends, to turn the helpless little vessel around.

Suddenly there was a loud crash—the boat had slammed into a rock! As it shattered to pieces, Ariana was flung into the water. She tried hard to swim towards the bank, but it was no use. She was being swept away by the powerful river, towards a place that would change her life forever. Ariana felt her head hit a rock, and then there was darkness as she passed out. Her friends were all swept away by the river, never to be seen again.

When Ariana opened her eyes, she found herself in a strange place. She was in a dark little hut, lying on the floor, covered by old rags. She sat up in a state of panic. Ariana could not remember what had happened. Her head throbbed with pain. Everything in the hut appeared blurry. There was a small log fire that, along with the rags, kept her warm. Ariana fell asleep.

It was many hours before she awoke again. This time she was greeted by a handsome young man, who was not from her part of the world. Ariana was beautiful and fair-skinned. This stranger who cared for her was tall, handsome and very dark.

"At last you are awake," he said to Ariana.

"Who are you, and where am I?" asked Ariana in a scared voice.

The young man looked at her with kind eyes and a warm smile and said, "My name is

Swaleem. I was out hunting with my friends and got caught in the terrible dark storm and I got lost. When I awoke, I found myself lying under the trees in a strange land. I wandered for days until I came across this little hut, which is now my home. I was out at the river one day and found you lying along the bank, with your eyes closed. I brought you here and cared for you, in the hope that some day you would open those beautiful eyes! I have sat here and watched you for what seems like forever, wondering how someone so beautiful could have been lost in this strange land."

Ariana replied, "I cannot remember who I am or where I have come from. I do not know how I got here. However, I am truly grateful to you for having saved my life."

Swaleem then said, "My father is the king of the great land of Mazarus. I know that he will be searching for me everywhere. But I know that this strange land is not part of our kingdom. I do not know if I will ever see my father again."

Ariana saw the tears gathering in the eyes of her saviour. She held out her hand towards his to comfort him. "I wish I could remember my home or my parents. I wish I could tell where I have come from. You are so kind. Only a very special person could do what you have done for me."

The prince replied, "At least neither of us is alone. Loneliness is the most difficult experience. I was alone for awhile before I found you. Having no one to talk to or share things with is the worst punishment one could suffer. My poor father, even in the midst of his thousands of subjects, is lonely right now, searching for me. He is feeling my pain, I know for sure. Since I was a little child, he has loved me and cared for me so much. I look into the night skies at the stars and wonder if he can be seeing them with me too."

Ariana could see that the prince was in much pain. "Swaleem, at least you can remember your home and your father. I can remember nothing. With your friendship, I have survived. Together, we are not lonely."

Several years went by. Swaleem and Ariana had fallen deeply in love with one another. They had grown to become best friends and lovers. The hut had been built up into a pretty little cottage. They had learned to live with nature. Everything they had came from the forests. They were happy. Swaleem still missed his father a lot. Ariana could not remember her home, her parents or anything else.

THE POWER OF LOVE: THE PARABLE OF ARIANA & SWALEEM

One day as Ariana and Swaleem sat on the bank of the river, they heard voices. This was the first time in years that they had heard human speech other than their own! They ran along the banks of the river towards the voices, to find a group of boats with at least twenty men travelling slowly in the relatively calm waters. They waved and invited them home.

The men docked their boats and came to the cottage. Ariana served them dinner and Swaleem told them of his experience. These men had heard of Swaleem's father and the kingdom of Mazarus.

"You are a long way from home, O Prince," said one of the travellers. "If you care to join us, we will take you back to your father."

Swaleem was elated. He looked at Ariana and said, "We can go home to my palace—you would absolutely love everything there."

Ariana, who was so happy for her beloved, said, "Yes, let us go with them to your home."

The next day Swaleem and Ariana walked away from their cottage to join their visitors for the boat journey home. They paused and looked back at their beautiful little house.

"This is our palace in the forests," Ariana said. "You are the king and I am your queen." Both felt sad to leave their home behind. But the prospect of what lay ahead of them was exciting!

After many days of travelling, Swaleem and Ariana arrived at the great palace of Mazarus. Swaleem's father was overjoyed to see his son again. He held his beloved child in his arms and wept. Swaleem then told him all about Ariana. The king welcomed her with great kindness. However, according to royal custom, Swaleem and Ariana could not be together any more.

The great joy of being reunited with his father was overshadowed by the pain of being separated from Ariana. She was given a room in the palace near the maids of honour. But Swaleem and Ariana could not see each other any more or enjoy the warmth of the love that they shared.

Swaleem pleaded with his father to allow him to marry Ariana. "I love her with all my heart, Father," he cried.

The king replied, "Swaleem, you are a prince. You are above everyone else. She is not your equal. How can you marry her?"

"Father, she is my equal," Swaleem pleaded. "She is me. She is my life. She is more important to me than all the riches of the kingdom. In all those years we shared in the forest, I was her husband and she was my wife. I was everything to her and she was everything to me. How can you say that we are not equal?"

The king then said, "Swaleem, you are of royal heritage. You are superior to all those around you. She is a lost girl, probably from the home of a peasant. She can be your slave, or your mistress if you insist. But she can never be your wife, for you are to become the Supreme King of this land. Your queen will be of royal blood. She will be from the palace of the Supreme. She will not be a commoner. That is our pride, my son."

Swaleem then said, "My beloved Father, the forest has taught me that everyone and everything is equal. All Creation is equal. None is above another. You are the king, but above you is a Greater King."

The father, who was getting irritated with his son, said, "Above me there is no Greater King. I am the Supreme one in this land, and so are you. We have power over everything. All beings bow to us. We are the Supreme, my son."

Swaleem replied, "If you were indeed so powerful, how come you could not save me from that dark thunderstorm? How come you could not find me, Father? I could have been dead, for all you knew. Where was your power then?"

The king had no words in reply to his son's piercing questions. He was enraged. He knew that his son would not be made to change his mind when it came to Ariana. That night he ordered the chief maid of honour to take Ariana away from the palace and escort her out of the kingdom. She was never to come back; that was his order.

Poor Ariana was terrified and heartbroken. As she walked away from the kingdom, she asked herself, "Where is my home? Where can I go? How can I leave my beloved one, who is the king of my Soul?"

She knew that she had to go away or else the wrath of the mighty king would fall upon her and her beloved prince. She travelled for days toward her home in the forest. She cried all along the way. Finally the tired, hungry and thirsty Ariana found her palace in the forest. Without Swaleem, it was not the same any more. But his memory kept her alive.

Swaleem was shattered when he learned of Ariana's departure. The matter had been kept secret from him for a long time. He sat in his room and stared at the sculpture on his wall of Ariana's beautiful face. He had had one of the most skilled artists in the kingdom produce this sculpture, which was an exact image of the beautiful Ariana.

Swaleem knew that his life in this palace was over. He had to find his beloved Ariana. In a strange way, he knew she was alive and he also knew where to find her. His father watched over him closely, but Swaleem was not stupid. He had learned a great deal about life.

All the fair-skinned people in the kingdom were slaves and people of a lower class. His father and he were worshipped by the people, for they were the ones who were believed to possess supernatural powers. Swaleem had learned that he was worthy of no worship. He had learned to worship his love and the Great One who caused the sun to rise each day and the trees to grow and the rivers to flow. His awareness was very different to that of his father. He knew that he had to leave.

Swaleem also knew that his father would come searching for him, therefore he wrote a note to his father in which he said that he was deeply unhappy and heartbroken because of the loss of his beloved Ariana. He said he had decided to take his own life, for this world had become unbearable for him. There was nothing left in it for him.

Quietly he slid out of the palace that night and set out on the journey to reunite with his beloved Ariana. In a strange way, he knew she was well and awaited him at their palace in the forest. After many days of travelling, he arrived at their beautiful cottage in the forest. He walked in quietly to find Ariana fast asleep. He kissed her on the forehead and she awoke!

This was the most joyous moment of their lives! They were together again. No riches of any kingdom could measure up against the treasure of their love.

Swaleem and Ariana lived together in great happiness and peace. They were blessed with lovely children, who were never to know that they were indeed princes and princesses. Swaleem and Ariana had dropped out of the pages of history!

Back in the kingdom of Mazarus, Swaleem's father mourned the death of his son. This was the most painful time of his life. He learned a lesson about the power of love. He learned that he was indeed not the most powerful king on Earth—he was simply a heartbroken father that had lost his only son and had no heir to his throne. He had never learned the lesson that was being taught to him by the Greater Being when he had lost his son the first time. Now it was all over.

A few years later, the great kingdom of Mazarus was invaded by King Saffiris of Tiberra. A huge battle took place; Mazarus was captured by Tiberra and Swaleem's father was taken prisoner. Brought into the presence of King Saffiris in chains, he faced his captor, who now sat on the throne in the great palace of Mazarus. King Saffiris said to his prisoner, "Bow before me, for I am your Master; I am the greatest king of all."

Swaleem's father obeyed and as he lowered his head, he remembered the words of his son, "My beloved Father, the forest has taught me that everyone and everything is equal. All Creation is equal. None is above another. You are the king, but above you is a Greater King."

Clearly King Saffiris was the greater king today. But he too was only a mortal above whom reigned the Greatest King of all! Swaleem's father had suffered great humiliation. He had lost his only son and now he had lost his kingdom. Where was his power? When he had ruled as king, he had been the centre of attraction. Now the sun had set for him; he had been overshadowed.

King Saffiris decided to spend some time at the palace of Mazarus before returning to Tiberra. One day as he explored the palace, he stopped at the room of Prince Swaleem. He felt a force that drew him into the room. There in front of him stood a sculpture of his beloved Ariana, the apple of his eye!

Ever since the day of the great storm, which in fact had caused the three rivers in Tiberra to split into four rivers, he had felt great pain as a result of the loss of his daughter. After searching for years, he had given her up for dead. The remains of her friends had been found, as had the remains of the boat. And now here he was, staring at a sculpture of his beloved Ariana, for whom he would have even given up his entire kingdom if that were the price that he had to pay to get her back. Tears rolled down his cheeks. He knelt before the sculpture and wept. He could not believe what he was seeing.

King Saffiris summoned Swaleem's father from prison and demanded to know where this sculpture had come from. The poor prisoner relayed the painful story of Swaleem and Ariana. Both fathers stared at each other, sharing one thing in common—a deep sense of loss and grief. King Saffiris said to the prisoner, "I would have given up my entire kingdom to get back my beloved Ariana."

The prisoner replied, "I was too drunk with the illusion of pride and power to learn anything from the loss of my son the first time. I clung to this illusion so tightly that even after I found him, I lost him again forever. All this time, I never learned to recognize Ariana and the special place she held in the heart of

Swaleem. You and I are both kings who are the centre of the universe for our people. For me, the sun has set. I have lost my kingdom and my most precious son."

King Saffiris replied, "For me, the sun set the day I lost my Ariana. There are things in our lives that are so precious. We never stop to recognize them, for we are too busy being the centres of our little universes. After hearing your story, all I can say is that I am glad that my dear Ariana found love in her life through Swaleem. For that, I will spare your life and let you rule over this land as my Emissary. Neither of us has won anything. We have both lost. . . ."

History recorded the death of Swaleem by suicide and the disappearance of Ariana into banishment. Yet the two lovers lived a wonderful life together in the forest. Neither of them ever became the centre of the universe, even in their little world in the forest. Such is the story of Swaleem and Ariana.

Received on October 20, 1997.

TWO

THE *S*AINT IN *C*ENTRAL *P*ARK: THE PARABLE OF THE CHIEF EXECUTIVE

There was once an executive called Barton who lived in New York City and worked hard at building up his large electronics company. He was an honest and conscientious individual, determined to succeed in this venture. His company was publicly listed on the stock exchange. The market for its shares, however, had dropped sharply to levels where he was unable to raise the capital he so badly needed.

One afternoon, after having taken more than fifty phone calls from irate investors and business associates, Barton decided he could

THE SAINT IN CENTRAL PARK: THE PARABLE OF THE CHIEF EXECUTIVE

not handle this any more! He stormed out of his office and took a cab to Central Park, his favourite hideout in the city. As he wandered through the park he saw a bench, where he decided to sit and allow himself to calm down.

A few moments later he saw a beautiful elderly Lady, dressed in a white robe, walking towards him. She walked with gentle, dignified steps; she looked like she could be about sixty-five years old. Her hair was grey and her eyes had a bright sparkle. A beautiful sandalwood scent surrounded her. Barton was taken aback by her radiance. She had a soft, affectionate presence that reminded him of his mother. This lady must be some kind of a Saint, he thought to himself. Then she stopped in front of him and, with a warm smile on her face, began speaking.

"Son, you look worried and upset. What could possibly be so wrong in your life to make you feel like this?"

Barton, somewhat humbled by her presence, said, "Lady, you look like you are enjoying your peaceful walk in the park. I don't want to bother you with my problems, but thanks for asking anyway!"

The Lady replied calmly, "Tell me what is on your mind, Son. Maybe I can help."

Barton felt comforted by her voice. He was generally a very closed person when it came to talking about his feelings. Yet he felt he could open up to this complete stranger who addressed him like she was his mother!

"Over the past few weeks I've been gravely concerned about my financial situation, compounded by the depressing performance of the stock markets," Barton let out. "I have faced much difficulty and pain. My shareholders have given me a lot of grief, too. All I do is listen to their frustrations and criticisms, which drain me mentally and emotionally. In the midst of all this, I find myself unable to think clearly. Hence, I am unable to find solutions to my crises. Today I left the office because I could not handle any more of this pain. I believe that it may be time for me to quit this business, because I am not happy at all!"

With a serious but understanding look on her face, the Lady replied, "Son, life is a multitude of Experiences. There are things we can control and then there are things we cannot control. The amount of commitment and effort that we put into our businesses, professions, relationships and all other activities clearly rests in our hands. However, we cannot control the outcome of our efforts. Success or failure is not in our hands."

The Lady continued, "Son, today as you ponder your problems, you do not know what events and solutions lie ahead of you. But, yesterday you did not know what was in store for you today! So why spend so much time and energy worrying about what is to happen next? All you can do is to try your best. If you make life a contest between success and defeat, you will feel highs and suffer lows. Son, think what it would be like to lead life in a constant form, taking in each Experience as it comes. Think of life where there is no success or failure—just Experience. People have made life to be one big competition. Does it need to be so?"

The Lady's eyes radiated with a special luminescence as she looked at Barton and continued, "Son, you must live each day as if it were your last. Then ask yourself how you feel about worldly success or failure."

Barton, who felt a wonderful new sense of energy, looked into the Lady's eyes and replied, "What you say makes a lot of sense. I have probably been too wrapped up in my problems to think clearly. I am terrified of failure. I spend so much of my time worrying about how people will feel about me if I fail. I try my hardest to keep everybody happy, from my employees to my investors, bankers and associates. Maybe that is why I have been unable to find the time to solve my problems."

Barton continued, "I feel so frustrated because I am unable to complete any task. I keep leaving behind loose ends wherever I go! Each moment of my day I fear what the next moment may bring. Each time the telephone rings, I shudder! I did not work this hard for all these years to put myself into such an unhappy situation. Clearly, I am not doing things right or else I wouldn't be in such a mess!"

The Lady smiled knowingly and replied, "Son, you must ask yourself the question, What success am I striving for? True success must be in the accomplishment of the purpose for which you were born. Where do you stand on that one? Have you thought about it? If your life were to come to an end today and by some special chance you were to be granted one more day, what would you do? What things would you take care of first? What would your list of priorities look like? Where would the business activities that consume sixteen hours of each day fit into this list? What would you want your obituary to say? Think about it, Son!"

The Lady continued, "You have always taken tomorrow for granted; you have automatically assumed that it would be there. This is where you often go wrong. You should aim to start each day by assuming that there will be no tomorrow. Remind yourself of that each morning as you get out of bed. Now make today's decisions accordingly. You will find that with this approach to life, you will accomplish a great deal. Your mess will gradually disappear. You will leave fewer loose ends in everything that you do. You will address the things that mean the most to you and in doing so, you will find happiness."

Barton pondered for a few moments what the Lady had said. He knew that every word reflected inner thoughts that had crossed his mind during quieter moments. Barton had pursued success in his business so hard that he had become oblivious to everything else in his life. At one time he had had a wife and a daughter—they no longer lived with him. He had had friends who cared about him, but in the relentless pursuit of his business goals, he had lost contact with them. Now he was all alone. Yet today, in Central Park of all places, he had heard the most profound words from a Lady whom he had never seen before!

"Ma'am, I do not know who you are or where you have come from," Barton said, "but you have given me much to think about. I will take the rest of the day off to reflect on your words. Clearly, what you are telling me to do is not easy. I have to change the way I think, and at the age of fifty, that can be difficult! I like your idea of listing my priorities because I know that there is much for me to correct. I have never given much thought to what my purpose in life is, but treating each day as if it were my last one may help me to discover a greater meaning in my life. I thank you for your counsel. By the way, Ma'am, how rude of me, I have not even introduced myself to you. My name is Barton."

The Lady smiled and replied, "Barton, it has been a pleasure meeting you. You are a fine man who means well. Change your ways and you will find the happiness you deserve! Don't worry too much about what the world thinks of you. Worry about what Barton thinks of himself! Farewell, Son, and may God bless you!"

As she started walking away, Barton felt a sudden sense of sadness. He cried out, "Ma'am, you never told me your name. Where can I find you if I need to speak to you?"

The Lady looked back with a warm smile on her face. With a soft, loving voice she replied, "You do not need to know my name. If you want to reach me, just think of me. . . ."

Received on September 9, 1994.

THREE

Making Wise Decisions:
The Parable of the Gold Trader

The Voice of Inspiration says to the Herald, *"Every step and every action in the life of a human being embodies a 'Contrast.' Life in this world is a dynamic process that leads toward an 'Equilibrium.' Therefore, each aspect of living carries more than one dimension, which is defineated by a Contrast. For example, an aspect of living that reflects 'Good' is countered by the Contrast of 'Bad.' Against every 'Plus', there is a Contrast of 'Minus.' When making a decision, one should seek to identify the Contrast in the situation and then direct one's actions toward the 'positive side' of the Contrast. This approach may help one in making good decisions. Most poor decisions result from straying towards the 'negative side' of the Contrast, or failing to recognize the Contrast itself!*

"When making decisions, one should consider that each side of the Contrast, positive or negative, carries Implications that may be simple or highly complex. These Implications usually influence the decision itself. By seeking to recognize the Contrast and thinking through as many of the Implications that exist on both sides as possible, one may be able to develop a Power of Reasoning, which could become a great asset.

"One of the most important purposes of human life is to seek Knowledge and gain Experience. Success or failure are less important than the Experience that is gained from every situation. In life, nothing is clearly black or white. Everything exists in shades of grey and this is why human beings have been blessed with the Intellect to make decisions within this intricate context. Understanding Contrasts, applying Experience and developing the Power of Reasoning to define and assess Implications are wonderful facets of this Intellect. Use them well. . . ."

MAKING WISE DECISIONS: THE PARABLE OF THE GOLD TRADER

There was once a businessman named Norman who sought to participate in the trading and refining of gold from West Africa. He came to this region with every intention of cooperating with the local people in order to build a healthy, flourishing enterprise. His business philosophy was based on building a two-way street between his company and the local people. Norman was a religious man who believed that through fair means he would be able to build a prosperous business for the benefit of all the people that were associated with him.

Little did Norman know that he had walked into a lion's den! In his first transaction he was asked to put down a 10-percent deposit to cover the transport costs, insurance and taxes for shipment of 100 kilograms of powdered gold to a precious-metals refinery in North America. Here the powder would be smelted, refined and poured into bullion bars. According to the agreement with the suppliers, the gold was to be entirely under Norman's custody from the moment it arrived in North America. He undertook to pay the remaining 90 percent of the shipment's value to the suppliers in West Africa as soon as settlement was received from the refinery. At the appointed date when the gold was to be shipped from West Africa, a false airway bill was issued to Norman by the shipping clerk at the airline, who allegedly disappeared with the merchandise. He was never to be seen again. All attention was focused on this one thief. But there's more. . . .

In a separate, parallel transaction, Norman got cheated by another thief who presented himself as the honourable chief of a local clan. This chief took money from Norman while portraying himself to be the leader of poor villagers who were in dire need to export gold that they had recovered from the river so they could buy rations and much needed machinery. Through the kindness of his heart, Norman trusted the chief and gave him several cash advances to pay the villagers whose gold he was purchasing. Once again, his money was stolen and no gold was delivered after several broken promises by the chief.

At the same time, Norman was being approached by more crooks with all kinds of gold-procurement opportunities. The web was growing fast. All along, Norman still believed that the chief was an honourable man who had been let down by others. Having lost twice, he agreed to recover his losses via a final transaction with the chief, but this time with great precautions put in place. A recovery formula for all previous losses was built into this transaction. At the appointed time of the transaction, Norman and the chief were ambushed by local police. Norman found himself under suspicion as an alleged drug-trafficker.

At the police station, poor Norman was detained long enough under questioning for the chief to make his way to the bank and withdraw all the money! The chief was conveniently allowed to get away. This third time, Norman found himself engulfed in a web that included the chief, the police, the assayers and the bankers, all of whom in their own respective ways contributed towards the theft and shared in the loot! Norman left West Africa frustrated, dejected and hurt, and deciding never to trade in gold ever again.

Norman's dear friend Alfred, who had watched the situation closely, asked himself, What went wrong? How did such a trusting, honest man get entangled in such a web? He thought of all the Contrasts that Norman had encountered. The first one lay in his decision to go to West Africa to trade in gold. The positive side of this Contrast was that Norman could have been able to build a good business and benefit from the profits. In addition, with his philosophy, the business would have positively impacted the lives of numerous local people. The negative side of the Contrast was that Norman would be deceived and robbed, which sadly enough happened to be the case.

Alternatively, the negative side of the Contrast could also have been that Norman may have encountered perfectly honest suppliers for the gold, whom he may have deceived and robbed! Alfred thought to himself that in this instance, Norman may have failed to recognize the Contrast itself, or he may have looked at the positive side and failed to look at all the Implications on the negative side.

Alfred then thought about the next set of Contrasts. When entering the first two gold-purchase transactions, Norman should have looked for the Contrasts. His contractual agreements should have considered the positive and the negative sides of these Contrasts. On the positive side, each party would have kept their side of the bargain. On the negative side, his deposit would have been stolen and the merchandise would never have shown up.

Alfred asked himself, Shouldn't Norman have built in special protections for his deposit? Perhaps. Norman may have argued that at some point in the deal, one of the parties had to put their trust on the line or else the transaction would not have occurred. Norman was a very trusting man, therefore he took the first risk! Alfred asked himself, Was that wise? The answer is not easy because Alfred was looking at the situation after the fact. Once again, Alfred thought that Norman may have failed to recognize the Contrasts or that he may have failed to look at all the Implications on the negative side.

Alfred then considered the third disaster. This time, when Norman made the mistake of dealing with the chief again, he clearly committed a fatal error in judgment because he had the Experience from the first two Contrasts to go by. While he had included safety mechanisms to prevent a repetition of the first two mistakes, he failed to recognize that the negative side of this third Contrast had many more possibilities! Norman found this out the hard way!

Alfred pondered Norman's decision to quit the gold-trading business altogether. After having learned so much and gained Experience the hard way, would it not have been better for Norman to try again, using an entirely different approach? He wondered what the Contrasts would look like under these circumstances.

One evening Alfred sat with Norman in front of a warm, cozy fire and the two friends reflected on the West African experience. They talked about each of the Contrasts that Norman had encountered. In the first two cases, Norman admitted that he had failed to recognize that the Contrasts ever existed! In the third case, Norman recognized the Contrast but failed to look at all the Implications on its negative side. He was too engrossed with the positive side and his desire to recover all his initial losses; this had clouded his judgment.

In his final decision—to leave the gold-trading business—Norman looked at the Contrast carefully and realized that there were far too many Implications on the negative side for him to tackle. Therefore he felt that the safer thing for him to do was to focus his time, attention and capital on a new business that had manageable Implications in its Contrasts. Alfred respected his friend's view, although he felt that Norman should have stayed in the game after learning the ropes.

Alfred then asked Norman a philosophical question. "Tell me, how did you learn to put so much trust in people? Each time I cautioned you about the people you were dealing with, you said to me that they were honourable people and that you had faith in them. Has this Experience shaken your confidence in human nature?"

Norman replied, "Alfred, I have always lived my life trusting in people. Many times I have succeeded because of this trust and many times I have failed. In every human being I see a Soul, which I believe comes from a very pure Origin. I believe that all Souls start from the 'good.' Hence, each being has a fundamental Essence which is 'good.' But the Mind, which is detached from the Essence, is where greed and treachery exist.

"My weakness in life has been that I have been able to readily recognize the Essence in everyone I meet, but I often fail to separate out the Mind. Therefore, while I see hope, love and sincerity in the Essence of each being, I often forget that a powerful Contrast exists at the level of their Mind. Where the Mind and Essence of a person are close to one another, the actions of the person reflect their Essence. Such people show love, warmth, compassion and purity in everything that they do. As the Mind and Essence drift further apart, there is an emptiness that becomes evident, which is usually accompanied by coldness, neglect and a lack of compassion. People whose Minds have lost touch with their Essence often find themselves dwelling on the negative side of the Contrast in most of their actions."

Norman continued. "My biggest problem in West Africa was that I failed to recognize the Contrasts when making decisions. Had I done so, I would have paid more attention to the Mind, rather than sensing the Essence alone. In this way, I may have made better decisions."

Alfred then said, "Norman, there is great wisdom in what you have just said. You see, the other extreme lies in where people only look at the Mind and its actions. They completely disregard or are unaware of the Essence. This breeds paranoia. Such people live in suspicion and are scared to do anything. They trust no one. This too is an unhealthy way of living because they fail to recognize the Contrast against which rests the Essence, which is inherently good."

Norman replied, "I believe that every relationship must be based on a 'Bond of Trust.' This bond comes from wisdom and Experience, which help us select the relationships we want to keep and how we want to manage them. Without trust, there can be no relationship. No matter how well we analyze Contrasts and their Implications, the final step in making a decision usually relies on Intuition, which is in fact the Voice of the Essence. If we listen to our Intuition, we will make fewer mistakes because Intuition comes from the Essence, which is always 'pure.' Intuition tells us how we 'feel' about a situation or a decision. Therefore, while care, wisdom and Experience can help lead us towards a rational decision, the final choice is usually made through Intuition. You see, Alfred, in every decision we make, there lies a special linkage between the Mind and the Essence. Intuition is one of those special linkages. But Intuition is easy to ignore or silence, especially if we don't like what it is telling us!"

As the two friends decided to wrap up for the day, Alfred said, "Norman, your outlook towards life and your Experience has taught me much. It would have been easy for me to mistake you for a fool when I looked at how you made your decisions in West Africa. Yet there is so much depth in your attitude towards life and towards people. None of us is perfect and as long as we learn from our successes and failures, we become better decision makers.

"Tomorrow, I am going to conduct an interesting exercise. I am going to look back and list all my successes and failures, which will include my friendships, relationships, business, employment and all other measurable aspects of my life. Then I will write the letter 'C' against each situation where I recognized the Contrast, and the letter 'N' against those situations where I failed to recognize the Contrast. I would like to see how often the letter 'N' appears against my failures!"

"Have fun with it, my dear friend!" Norman replied. "After returning from West Africa I did the very same exercise. My conclusions were most revealing!"

Received on March 31, 1996.

FOUR

THE *A*LPS:
A SYMBOL OF HUMILITY

It was a bright sunny day and the Angels Cyrus and Luminus decided to travel to the Swiss Alps, which was their favourite place on Earth. From time to time they liked to visit the natural springs and enjoy the fresh, crystal-clear water. They loved playing in the meadows, where rare flowers and herbs grew amidst the luscious green grass. Cyrus looked at the flower-filled valley and complained, "If only people knew how precious these flowers and herbs are! They can cure the worst of illnesses. They grow here in the valleys and are seldom noticed. Think of how much time, money and energy is spent by people developing and taking dangerous chemicals to cure their simple illnesses."

Luminus agreed. "The most complex of problems that people face can be solved by the simplest of things. These herbs and flowers were placed here and in many other places in the world to help protect and cure humanity from illnesses. Yet they have been ignored and replaced by chemicals, which only cause more new illnesses! Here in our favourite Alps lie many simple solutions, from things that can be seen to symbols that cannot be seen."

Cyrus replied, "I have heard that the Alps represent a great symbol of Humility and I have often wondered how."

Luminus answered, "I too have heard that from the other Angels, but I do not know why! We must try to discover the answer. We must ask the Voice of Inspiration to explain this to us. . . ."

As Cyrus and Luminus flew by Mont Blanc they marvelled at the snow-capped peaks that stood tall and strong, with sharp edges drawing lines that ran straight into the sky. This entire range of mountains rested on a single, long, solid base from which arose many peaks.

Cyrus and Luminus halted their flight as they heard the Voice of Inspiration say to them,

"Angels, look at the snow that covers the peaks of these mountains! What do you see?"

The Angels could see that the lower parts of the Alps were green and grey in colour. Yet the peaks were all white. The Voice of Inspiration then said, *"You see, Angels, the snow on the peaks of the mountains is a symbol of their Humility. Even the tallest mountains cover their heads out of respect for their Origin (Creator). I hope that answers your question."*

The Voice of Inspiration continued. *"Angels, when you last visited the mosques in Arabia, the synagogues in Israel and the temples in India, you asked why Muslims, Jews, Sikhs and people of most faiths cover their heads before they enter their place of prayer. The answer is simple and it lies here in one of the symbols of the Alps. You see, Angels, the head of the human being is like the peak of the mountain. It is the focal point from which all energies radiate throughout the body. It is the cradle in which rests the Intellect. Therefore when people come before their Origin in prayer, they cover their heads out of Humility, respect and submission, just like the snow-capped peaks of the Alps. This is the truth behind the act that is practised by so many. . . ."*

After listening intently as the Voice of Inspiration answered their question, the Angels

THE ALPS: A SYMBOL OF HUMILITY

continued their flight over the Alps. Cyrus said to Luminus, "The analogy between the mountain and the human being is truly a compliment to humanity. As mountains become taller, their snow covers become larger and denser. Therefore, when people rise higher in whatever they do, they should become more humble, like the mountains."

Luminus replied, "That is not always the case in this world! Pride and vanity usually take over. Cyrus, I believe that if Humility does not reach people as they rise to greatness, they will become like the jagged peaks that erode in the rain, sun and storms, until they become so small that the snow can never cover them again! Human history is filled with examples of this, but little has been learned. Nothing has changed!"

Cyrus pointed to the Alps and said, "Behold, Luminus! Look at the snow-capped peaks. While they stand tall and strong, they display the Humility that must go with this strength. From this Humility comes Mercy, for as the snow melts, it yields crystal-clear water that runs down the sides of the mountain to nourish everything that it touches!

"Luminus, look at the reflection of the brilliant rays of the Sun as they bounce off the snow-capped peaks!" Cyrus continued. "It is almost as if there is a glow of Light that lives on such peaks."

Luminus replied, "These special symbols of Humility, Mercy and Light that the Alps portray are unfortunately missed by humanity. Therefore, they achieve far less than their true potential. Cyrus, when we look around the world, we can only see a precious few mountain peaks that are covered with snow all the year round. For every snow-capped peak, there are a hundred barren hills! Such is the truth about human life."

Cyrus looked down at the carpet of snow and responded, "Luminus, do not forget that it is the peaks of mountains that get noticed the most, because they stand out amidst everything. Such is the greatness of humanity. If there is Humility within this greatness, then there will be Mercy and Light."

Luminus replied, "Everything you say is true, dear Cyrus! But for people to achieve greatness, they need to learn from these mountains which have been placed on the Earth as beacons of understanding. In them lie knowledge and symbols of so many aspects of human life. . . ."

Received on February 19, 1995.

FIVE

*F*EAR:

THE PARABLE OF THE SLAVE

The Voice of Inspiration says to the Herald: *"Fear comes from one's inability to embrace the unknown. Fear stems from lack of Faith. Faith adds a dimension of 'knowing' to the 'unknown.' Trust and Hope are essential elements of Faith. At the Dawn of Life, at birth, one starts with 100 percent of the unknown that lies ahead of oneself. At the Dusk of Life, at death, one leaves with 100 percent knowledge, for there are no unknowns. In between the Dawn and the Dusk resides Fear. If Dawn starts with Trust and Hope, then Faith leads one successfully to the Dusk. However, when Faith, Trust and Hope are overcome by one's inability to embrace the unknown, one lives in a constant state of Fear. . . ."*

One dark starry night, King Marcus sat with his philosopher Juan in the gardens of the royal palace, talking about a case that the king had to judge the next day. By nature, King Marcus was paranoid. He trusted no one and assumed the worst in every situation. Needless to say, he waged many wars against his neighbours, as well as in kingdoms that were too far away to cause him any harm. His military advisors took advantage of his paranoia by instigating rumours of hostile intentions by his neighbours, so that they could personally benefit from the looting and plundering that usually accompanied Marcus's attacks. King Marcus was now fifty years old and the most powerful king in his region. He had no friends and preferred to be alone most of the time.

This evening he was seeking the counsel of Juan on the case of Azam, the slave who had bought his freedom through hard work and was establishing himself as a successful merchant in the land. Azam's enemies had plotted to destroy his little enterprise and discredit him to the point where he could be enslaved again. They set up a trade with Azam: six sacks of his good rice in exchange for six gold coins. Poor, unsuspecting Azam delivered his rice and collected his six coins. He did not know that his enemies had replaced the good sacks of rice in his store with poorest-quality rice—rice that would not even be fed to the chickens! There were many witnesses to this transaction.

As Azam was walking back to his home, he was arrested by the King's soldiers and charged with fraud and theft. He was immediately imprisoned, awaiting trial. His enemies arranged to have his case heard by the king himself because they wanted to set an example for all slaves who sought their freedom. The king did not know anything about all this.

The king asked Juan, "Tell me about the slave Azam. Where is he from and why is he being charged with fraud and theft?"

Juan replied, "Azam was brought to our land by the Arab traders. I believe he is from West Africa. He was picked up by the slave traders in his village ten years ago, when he was thirteen years old. He was bought from the traders by Isaac, the corn miller. Isaac is an unusual man. He told Azam that he could earn his freedom if he milled a thousand sacks of corn every year for seven years."

Marcus interjected, "That is impossible! No man can mill a thousand sacks per year!"

"That is indeed correct," Juan replied. "But young Azam was so determined to become a free man that he worked without stopping for the full seven years. He hardly slept during the night and toiled throughout the day. At the end of the seven years, Isaac kept his word and freed Azam. This caused the people in the kingdom, when they heard about it, to become very upset. To make matters worse, Azam decided to become a rice trader. In some strange way, he began to prosper more than his competitors. Of course, now we can see a possible reason why! He probably profited by selling poor-quality rice at prices deserving much better quality."

"That is despicable!" King Marcus said. "If he did that, he should pay for it! But Juan, I ask you, how could a man with such a strong will participate in such fraudulent activities? Do you not think that his seven years of hard labour would have taught him to keep out of trouble? If he could buy his freedom at such a price, do you not think this man understands the concept of value? There is something here that does not meet the eye."

"Yes, it does seem strange," Juan replied, "but he was caught red-handed. There were many witnesses!"

King Marcus then said, "How should I judge him tomorrow?"

"You will need to know the truth before you can judge him," Juan replied. "Although he was caught red-handed, there may be a truth that remains unknown. Until you know the unknown, how can you judge him?"

King Marcus was confused by this statement. He asked the philosopher, "How can there be an unknown? The facts are quite clear. All I need to do now is to pass judgment. This is what I do in all situations. I decide what is the truth and I act accordingly. I do not like to waste time."

Juan replied, "At the risk of offending you, my dear King, I must disagree. How many times have you attacked our neighbours when you simply thought that their intentions were hostile? You did not know for sure what their intentions were. You may recall that over the past thirty battles, you were the one that attacked first twenty-nine times! If the truth as you perceived it were correct, we would have been attacked more than once!"

King Marcus did not like what he was hearing. "Our neighbours could not be trusted!" he shouted. "They were always plotting against me. I had to eliminate them!"

Juan, who knew his situation was precarious, said, "That is true, O Beloved King. But how about the other twenty battles you waged against kingdoms that were too far away to affect us?"

The king replied, "I heard of their intentions through my informants. They posed a threat, so I had to attack!"

"How do you know that your informants were telling the truth?" Juan asked. "From what I have seen, we have waged wars against peaceful people all the time. I believe that you attacked them because of what you did not know rather than because of what you had heard. Surely you must have wondered what the truth really was."

"To me they represented the unknown," the king replied. "I did not trust any of them. Therefore I had to attack them lest they should decide to attack me. Believe me, Juan, I do not enjoy war. The battlefield terrifies me! But I have to do what is necessary."

"You attacked everyone out of Fear, O Beloved King," Juan then said. "You could not accept the unknown and this increased your Fear! Even in the battlefield you fought out of Fear because you knew not what would happen next!"

Marcus was furious. He screamed, "Juan, you could pay for this insolence with your life! How dare you call me a coward!"

Poor Juan, now shaken, replied, "I am sorry if I have offended you, my Great King. I never suggested that you were a coward. I see a great difference between Fear and cowardice. Fear rests in all of us. It causes us to attack or to run. He that runs is a coward. You, my Great King, are not a coward—this I can attest to with my life!"

The king was soothed by this remark. "Juan, I cannot deny that I feel Fear in everything I do; it is with me all the time," he said. "When I do not know what lies ahead, it dominates me. But I also have great courage, for I have no hesitation in facing my enemy. And Juan, you know well that I have a great number of enemies who would do anything to bring my kingdom down."

The philosopher replied, "Yes, O Great King, you are so right. I too lived in Fear until one day I realized that every moment of my life that lay ahead of me was an unknown. I learned to accept the unknown. Since then I have not felt the pains of Fear. In a strange way, by accepting the unknown, I learned to Trust and this gave me a completely different outlook towards myself, my neighbours and everyone that I came in contact with. I was not suspicious any more and people felt more relaxed being with me. You see, O Great King, I do not believe that you have as many enemies as you think. Fear creates enemies in our minds. As long as we Fear, our enemies exist. As soon as we stop Fearing, they disappear!"

"You are right, Juan," King Marcus observed. "All my life I have found great difficulty in dealing with the unknown. Through my Fear I have destroyed a great deal. I have banished people from the kingdom because I suspected their intentions were no good. Each time I speak to my military advisors, I feel my heart pounding against my chest as I hear about more new enemies. Each time I go to battle, my stomach churns with Fear of losing or being killed. It is a horrible feeling, Juan, as I am sure you know. The fact that you have the courage to be so frank with me tells me that you have no Fear. I can learn a great deal from you."

"O Great King, our religion teaches us to have Faith," Juan commented, "and we often wonder what that means. Behind all our elaborate rituals lies a simple concept of Belief. This Belief can be in God, Nature, our friends, loved ones or ourselves. It really does not matter. But Believing means embracing the unknown. Fear comes from our inability to embrace the unknown."

King Marcus had learned much from the philosopher that evening. The next morning Juan joined him at the trial of the slave Azam. The court was filled with spectators. King Marcus was surprised with the size of the turnout at this trial. It made him curious. After the charges were read to Azam, the king asked him, "Young Azam, what do you wish to say in your defence to these grave charges?"

The slave replied, "O mighty King Marcus, I am innocent. I have committed no fraud. The night before the transaction, my store was filled with rice of the best quality. When I did the trade for the six gold coins, I genuinely believed that I had delivered the best of my product. I was astonished to find that the sacks had been switched. As a matter of fact, the people from whom I purchase my rice will attest to the fact that I only buy the best of their produce. This is why I have enjoyed success in my trading."

"Are you suggesting that someone stole your good rice and replaced it with the rubbish that you traded that day?" the king asked. "This is a very serious allegation you make, Azam!"

The slave replied, "Your Majesty, I cannot say for sure what happened because I was not present to witness the change of sacks. Therefore I cannot explain how it happened. But what I do know for sure is that I did not buy, nor did I own, the poor-quality rice."

"I have heard about how you bought your freedom through hard work," the king then said. "Surely during the seven years that you toiled for Isaac, you never really knew that he would indeed keep his word, did you?"

Azam replied, "No, Your Majesty, I didn't. But I trusted him to keep his word."

The king then asked, "How could you have placed seven years of your life in Isaac's hands purely on Trust? Where did you learn to Trust like this?"

The slave replied, "Your Majesty, one day when I was thirteen years old, I was playing with my father outside our hut as my mother and sisters watched. We were a happy family. Then from behind the bushes appeared the slave catchers, with their daggers and ropes. As they tried to catch me, my father came to my rescue and one of the ruthless catchers stuck a dagger in his heart. I rushed to hold my dying father's head in my arms but I was torn way by the strong hands of my captors. My mother and sisters were also taken away as slaves and I have never seen them since. Your Majesty, in one brief moment, my entire world came to an end.

"The morning before I was captured, I had no idea of the terrible things that would happen to me in a few hours. After I was captured I did not know where I was going to be taken or what I was going to do. I was terrified. Each time a leaf moved in the wind, my heart would stop with Fear! But I learned to accept that whatever lay ahead of me was a journey that would shape my life. This journey was full of unknowns. As I thought about it, my entire life was an unknown from the moment I was born. As I learned to embrace the unknown, I was no longer afraid. As I learned to Trust and have Faith in God, I began to overcome my Fear. Your Majesty, I am all alone in this world and therefore I have learned to be my own best friend. I have learned to Trust myself and this has helped me to Trust others. This is why I could Trust Isaac's word so freely."

King Marcus was dumbfounded with the story of the slave. "Azam, you are a remarkable man!" he said. "For a person who has suffered such disruptions and violence in his life, I would have thought that every moment of your day and night would be filled with Fear. Yet here you are, calm and confident, sharing with us all the strength of your Trust. You must truly have great Faith in God and yourself. A man like you is too solid in character to commit the frauds that you have been accused of! I therefore pronounce you a free man!"

Azam, his eyes filled with tears, said to the king, "Your Majesty, I am truly grateful to you for granting me my freedom. May God bless you!"

"Young Azam, I am truly grateful to you," the king replied, "for you have taught me how to free myself from my Fears!"

King Marcus then looked at Juan, the philosopher, and smiled. Juan smiled back.

"O Great King Marcus," Juan began. "No philosopher could ever explain so beautifully the special place that Faith, Trust and Hope should hold in our hearts. Fate dealt the harshest of cards to Azam, yet look where the strength of his Faith has brought him. Behold, my Great King, we have much to correct!"

Received on March 11, 1995.

SIX

Detachment: The Parable of the Swiss Merchant

The Voice of Inspiration says to the Herald, *"'Detachment' is an essential aspect of one's existence. It brings freedom and allows one to seek and discover great strengths, both in the material and spiritual dimensions. Write about the story of Alfred, the Swiss merchant, and his encounter with the Sun, for there is much to be learned. . . ."*

It was a warm summer day in Zürich when Alfred, a famous dealer in fine Swiss watches, rushed to the airport to catch a flight to Johannesburg for a meeting with some of his important customers. Alfred was a successful businessman. He had worked hard over the past twelve years to build his enterprise, for this was his dream. He had built markets for his products all over the world and he enjoyed a great deal of respect from the business community wherever he operated.

Alfred's business activities kept him very busy, and as a result he spent little time with his wife Emily and his fifteen-year-old daughter, Suzanne. He sometimes wondered whether losing this precious time with his family was indeed worth the success he enjoyed in business. Alfred was almost forty years old and it would not be long before Suzanne would be ready to leave home for college in America. In the earlier years of their marriage Alfred and Emily had been very close, but now they were drifting further apart each day because they made so little time for one another. They had little left in common except for Suzanne. When they were alone, they did not know what to say to each other any more.

As Alfred's plane lifted off from the runway, he noticed the large red Sun setting against the backdrop of the magnificent Swiss Alps. It was so beautiful and radiant that all he wanted to do was to stare at it. He felt a special sense of warmth as the rays of the Sun began to penetrate his heart and Soul. He had never felt this way before! He wanted this wonderful experience to go on forever, but unfortunately, much to his dismay, the plane began to take a sharp turn away from the Sun. Alfred felt a sudden, deep sense of loss. He cried out to the Sun, "Don't leave me, O beautiful Sun! Don't go away from me—please!" But the plane continued to turn until he could not see the Sun any more. He felt cheated and disappointed.

Then a strange thing happened—he heard the Sun call out in return to him. *"My dear Alfred, I am here,"* It said. *"I am still here, as I have always been! I have not left you. It is you that turned away from me. I am still here for you."*

Alfred felt helpless and upset, for he so desperately wanted to be with the beautiful setting Sun. He replied, "O Beloved Sun, I did not turn away from you out of choice—I have no choice! I do not control the plane; I am but a mere passenger on it! I never wanted to turn away from you."

The glorious Sun watched as Alfred's plane moved away and replied, *"I am still here for you, Alfred. It is true that you do not direct the course of the plane. You are only but a passenger. You are driven by circumstances now. But Alfred, at every point in your life, you have a choice that you can make. It is only after you have made this choice that circumstances take over. Think—did you have a choice whether to board the plane in Zürich or not? You made the conscious decision to board the plane and now you do not have any control over what happens next. Such is the flow of your life. In so many ways I am no different than Emily and Suzanne, from whom you have turned away too! However, in their case you were not on a plane that took you away. You had much more control over your actions!*

Alfred sat quietly and thought about what the Sun had said to him. This was the first time in his life that he was truly beginning to experience a sense of loss. Until today, Alfred had been an ambitious go-getter; he stopped at nothing to reach his ambitions. He found joy in his business accomplishments. But now, on this flight, he began to realize that all his accomplishments meant very little. For a few moments, he had felt the special rays of the Sun. He knew that the Sun would rise and set the next day and that he could seek its warmth then. But he could no longer wait until tomorrow. He wanted the plane to turn towards the Sun, which was now quickly beginning to fade into the horizon. He thought of Emily and Suzanne, who were also as warm and beautiful as the rays of the setting Sun, but in all these years he had not noticed them!

The Sun once again spoke to Alfred. *"It is time for you to learn an important lesson today. All your life you have been obsessed by your ambitions and your material well-being. During this period some wonderful moments of love, affection and warmth have passed you by, without your being aware if it. Today you must learn the importance of Detachment. It is a special word. You have been too Attached to your business and material possessions. Therefore you missed out on Emily and Suzanne. If you Detach yourself from your business and material activities for a certain amount of time each day, you will begin to discover and become Attached to your loved ones. In this, you will find much happiness."*

The Sun continued, *"Alfred, now ask yourself, Why were you born? What is your purpose in life? Who are you? Where is the real Alfred? Of course, these are difficult questions because you have to search deep within yourself for the answers. You need to Detach yourself from everything else and focus your mind and spirit on these important questions. You need to discover the real Alfred and become Attached to him. This can only be achieved through Detachment from all your material distractions.*

"Let me give you a simple example of a bee in the garden. There is a special flower in this garden, called Sapira, that only blossoms for twenty-four hours and then it dies. The bee seeks to pollinate Sapira, for this is the purpose of its life. But in the garden there are so many other flowers that attract the bee. Once it rests on any one of them, it gets consumed with enjoying their nectar—it becomes 'Attached.' It loses sight of the fact that Sapira still remains to be found in the midst of its blossom and pollinated. If the bee is to achieve its purpose in life, it needs to Detach itself from all the other flowers in the garden until it has found Sapira. Remember that if it cannot break free from the other flowers, Sapira may blossom and die and the bee may never find it again, no matter how hard it tries!"

The Sun continued, *"You see, Alfred, Detachment brings freedom. This freedom allows you to flow like water towards whatever it is that you desire. If you are successful in finding your true Self, you will find immense peace and joy. This experience will be a lot deeper and more powerful than your discovery and Attachment with Emily and Suzanne. This experience will be one of Enlightenment."*

DETACHMENT: THE PARABLE OF THE SWISS MERCHANT

Alfred pondered what he had heard. Clearly he was beginning to learn that to achieve Attachment with whatever he desired, he would have to Detach himself from everything else for an appropriate period of time. He asked the question, "What is an appropriate period of time?"

In the distance he heard the Sun reply, *"You will know what the appropriate period of time is. Depending on what you are seeking to achieve, the appropriate period of time could be as short as a few minutes or it could be as long as a lifetime!"*

From that day on, Alfred's life changed forever. He found a new bond with Emily and Suzanne. He found great peace as a result of his inner search for his true Self. He found contentment and happiness in all that he did, because he had learned to achieve a balance between Attachment and Detachment. He carved out "new time" in his days and in his nights, because he had gained the ability to flow through events like water, with complete freedom and flexibility. Ironically his business flourished immensely as well, as a result of this special personal metamorphosis.

One evening several years later Alfred looked up at the setting Sun and said, "O beloved Sun, you have taught me to achieve my very best, with such little effort!"

The Sun smiled and replied, *"My dear Alfred, how do you think I manage to keep the Earth and all Creation on it warm, happy, energized and loved . . . ?"*

Received on June 4, 1996.

SEVEN

THE *R*AINDROP AND THE *B*LADE OF *G*RASS: A PARABLE OF LIFE CYCLES

There was once a Droplet of water that fell from the sky in a rain shower, onto a green field where healthy blades of grass formed a carpet over the soil. As it landed on the Grass, it gasped a sigh of relief and said, "I am on land again—thank Heaven!"

The Grass replied, *"Welcome, dear Droplet. I have awaited you so long; at last you are here!"*

The Droplet looked across the field and saw hundreds and thousands of other little Droplets dancing playfully on their blades of Grass. This was a moment of rejoicing and jubilation for these precious little drops of water, because they had finally landed safely in the grass field. In the distance there was a barren patch of soil; it looked like a desert in the midst of the green fields. As more raindrops fell to the ground, the less fortunate ones kept landing on the barren patch of soil, which thirstily soaked them up!

The Droplet said to the Grass, "Thank God I landed on you and not on the barren patch, for at least with you I am in the sunlight. I feel sad for those poor Droplets that have landed out there on the barren soil, for they have been plunged into darkness!"

The Grass replied, *"You are lucky, my dear Friend. As each day goes by, I am visited by Droplet after Droplet. For those that land on me, I show them Love and cradle them in my gentle being. Then, when the sun shines, they go away, back into the skies. Oh yes, I have seen Droplets that have sunk into darkness under the soil. I have picked them up with my roots and set them free through my leaves! I have heard their stories and, believe me, they are profound! I have spoken to Droplets that have had to land in deserts and remain in darkness for what seemed like eternity, until some day they could be set free again.*

"I have also hosted Droplets like you, who rest on me and leave again in the sunshine.

THE RAINDROP AND THE BLADE OF GRASS: A PARABLE OF LIFE CYCLES

Tomorrow I can watch you sail in the sky with the clouds again and my heart will leap with joy each time you pass over me. My dear Friend, I know that your journey is long and difficult. You fall from the sky and land in places that are destined for you. Never forget that you will only fall in places where your 'Karma' (deeds/actions) takes you."

The Grass continued, *"My dear Friend, ask yourself how many cycles you have been through. How many times have you come to the land and then left again? How many types of circumstances have you experienced? You have seen pain, sorrow and joy. You have been free and you have also been encaged. You have been in the light and you have also been plunged into darkness. In the midst of this darkness there have been roots of trees and Grass that have helped you out and set you free again!"*

The Grass continued, *"O dear Droplet, ask yourself where you started from and where you are going. There was a time when you were the Ocean. You were one with Infinity. You were powerful and majestic. Now you are on a special journey. While the Ocean and you are one, your power is now hidden. It has been transformed from the obvious to the subtle. Cycle after cycle, you strive to return to the Ocean. But before you can get there, there is much that you must accomplish. There are plants you must feed. There is thirst that you must quench. There are places that you must cool. There are feet that you must kiss when you are a dewdrop. There is light that you must reflect, for indeed there is a period when you must sparkle. Your actions at each stage of your journey determine where you go next. For you, O Beloved Droplet, it is my prayer that you rise in the sky again and that you travel in the cloud that will carry you to the Ocean, your Home. If this is not to be, then I pray that the cloud may take you to the River, through which you may reach the Ocean. Your Creator has laid forth so many Rivers to carry precious Droplets like you to the Ocean. I pray that you may find your River. You must strive for nothing less. Do not be plunged into darkness, for you know the pain of darkness. Do not wander needlessly or keep coming to the land without getting closer to the River, for that is wasting your precious life cycles. I cannot tell you how many cycles you have left, but I can say that some of them will be long, dark and painful, while others will be joyous and fulfilling. Such is the beauty of your journey."*

The Grass continued, *"I see the sun is shining again. In a few moments you will depart. I am grateful for having been granted the opportunity of being with you for this brief* period. I have passed on to you my Knowledge. I have shared with you reflections that will lead you to the Ocean. O dear Friend, I hope you have learned something from me. If you haven't, then I will be just another blade of Grass that sheltered you for a brief few moments. On the other hand, if you have learned something from me, then I believe your next stop is the River, or—if you are fortunate —the Ocean. In that case, you will certainly know who I am!"

Received on March 21, 1995.

EIGHT

THE *M*ESSAGE OF *R*EINCARNATION: THE PARABLE OF TARA

The Voice of Inspiration says to the Herald, *"In the plane of the Eternal exist Souls who are governed by neither time nor space. They exist purely within a simple State of Being. This is a State that one cannot describe in physical terms. They may take physical forms as needed for the accomplishment of their journey. All Souls just Be and it is only when a physical form is taken that outward and visible expressions begin to manifest. O Herald, write about the story of Tara, which reveals an important message on reincarnation. . . ."*

There is a Soul who is called Tara, who exists peacefully in the State of the Eternal. The only reason we refer to this Soul as Tara is in order to give it identity in a form that we understand. Tara is now choosing to take a physical form.

The Scroll of Tara's journey so far, which identifies all experiences and deeds, both good and bad, is clearly recited within Tara in the form of Thought. On the basis of this Scroll, which is very precise, Tara chooses to be born as a girl in Burma. Her parents are to be a poor farmer and his wife. Her home is to be a thatched grass hut.

Tara's goal is to fulfill all the debts that remain outstanding as per the Scroll of her Eternal Journey. She is given a specific duration within which her aims are to be fulfilled. Within the Eternal State, Tara also strongly desires to rise and merge into the Light of her Creator. Throughout her Eternal Journey she has been unable to do so, because in each life form she has suffered distractions that have led her away from her goals. In this lifetime, Tara aims to satisfy the outstanding matters in the Scroll, pay her dues, heal the hurts that she has caused, collect what has been owing to her and rise into the Light of Creation.

Why did Tara choose Burma? Why did she choose to become a girl? Why did she elect to become the daughter of the peasant farmer and his wife? Where does she intend to go from here, and why? The answers to these questions lie in events and experiences that Tara has been through over many, many life cycles and forms. Each time a Soul takes a physical form, it hopes that it may never ever have to take a physical form again. However, once birth occurs in the material plane, all is forgotten.

The date is May 18, 1664. Tara is born! Her mother has been through a very painful pregnancy. What a relief it is to have this beautiful baby girl spring out of her weak body! Her father rejoices at the birth of his first daughter. Tara has two older brothers. This is a day of great excitement for this little Burmese family.

The village has been suffering a severe drought. On the day Tara is born, however, the rain clouds pour their contents generously over all the farms. "This little girl has brought us good luck," says Tara's father, Chian.

The years went by and Tara began to grow into a fine young lady. She was beautiful and was loved by everybody in the village. She gave love and care freely and her warmth lit the hearts of all those around her. She was indeed a blessing to the entire village. In lives gone by, Tara had taken much from people. She had been vain and had caused much pain and hurt to those around her. Now she had returned to heal and to give back. Her parents, family and members of the village had all been a part of the outstanding debt that she had to settle.

In her new physical form, Tara had forgotten her true identity. She did not have a clue as to why she was living in this world. Her good fortune was that she consciously gave freely to all. In this way, while she was not fully aware, she kept fulfilling her purpose for this lifetime.

One afternoon Tara was walking through the fields on her way home. As she walked through thick bushes, she heard the screaming of a child. She dropped her pot of water and ran to where the noise was coming from. A three-year-old girl was being attacked by a deadly cobra! The little girl was terrified and the black snake was all but ready to bite her! Tara flung herself at the snake in order to save the child. She felt a sharp burning sensation in her left thigh, then her whole body seemed on fire. She had been bitten and she thought that her life was about to end.

Her vision began to turn blurry. She looked at the little girl that she had just saved from the snake, but she could not really see this child. Instead, she found herself looking at a beautiful young maiden, who was waving at her. She immediately recognized who this maiden was! It was her closest friend in one of her previous lives, who had died while in Tara's care!

Tara had been entrusted to look after her friend as they went out to catch fish in the river. While the girls sat by the river with their fishing rods in the water, an argument broke out over a young man that both girls loved. In a state of rage, Tara, who was the older and stronger of the two, pushed her friend into the river. The fast-flowing water quickly carried the poor girl away. Her body was found several days later at the bottom of a waterfall!

Tara had never ever told anyone the truth about what had happened. This little girl that she had just saved was the very same friend whose life Tara had once taken! In the midst of all her pain, Tara prayed to God with gratitude for having helped her to settle this major debt. In her delirious state, she could see glimpses of a bright, warm Light that appeared in the distance. Pink and white petals fell from the sky in front of this Light. Bright as it was, it did not dazzle Tara.

The next thing she remembered was waking up in the lap of an old Saint. The Saint had seen what had happened and rushed to Tara's rescue. He had tied a cloth tightly around her thigh to prevent the spread of the poison. He even bit into her thigh to suck out whatever poison he could. As all of this happened, the little three-year-old girl just watched. Through the help of the Saint, Tara had been saved. But half of her body had been instantly paralyzed.

The villagers found her lying in the bush with the little girl sitting next to her. There was no Saint to be seen—He had vanished! Who was He, Tara wondered? She tried to explain to the villagers what had happened, but the words could not come out of her mouth. The little girl was too young to explain what she had seen, therefore this experience remained a mystery for the villagers. It was as much a mystery as what had happened to Tara's friend in her previous life who had been washed away in the river. In both cases, Tara was the only one who really knew what had happened. She often remembered the face of the Saint. He had come out of that beautiful Light to save her. Who was He? she wondered.

As the years went by, Tara was married to the son of one of the poorest families in the village. She could no longer walk by herself. She needed others to help her walk, bathe and feed herself. She was completely paralyzed. It was a miracle that her husband had agreed to marry her in such a state! This too had been because of a debt that she had to collect from him, as was written in his and her Scrolls. Her husband was very kind to her and loved her very much indeed. He became her lover, her mother, her father—everything to her. She was totally dependent on him, but at no time did she feel sad about it. Her taking from him felt right for both of them, for indeed it was in their Scrolls.

After two years of marriage, a very special spiritual bond was bestowed upon Tara. A new Soul was merged into hers; she was to become a mother. The Soul of her child had united with her own Soul, and the Soul of her child was no stranger to her. This was indeed the Soul of her brother in a previous life, who had committed suicide at the age of eighteen.

When one commits suicide, one's Soul dwells in a state of "no belonging." It no longer has a physical form to give it material expression. It does not belong within the Eternal State, either. It is wandering and lost. Tara had had a lot to do with her brother's suicide. Before her birth, while in her Soul state, Tara could clearly see and feel the pain that her brother's Soul was suffering. She pleaded with her Creator to give her brother a physical form so as to help him to get out of the state of wandering and back into the Abode of Peace, where she prayed he would belong. This was one of the last outstanding matters that Tara had to settle.

When the snake had bitten her, she had been shown glimpses of the Light of Creation that she so dearly yearned to unite with. Now the Saint who had helped her appeared before her again and said, *"My dear Tara, I have granted you your wish to give your brother a second chance. You will give birth to him. Whilst his Soul has merged into yours, you will impart to him the wisdom, peace, love and warmth that you now possess. This will help him in his life to come, for immense storms lie ahead of him to overcome."*

In her ninth month of pregnancy, Tara went into labour in the early hours of the morning. She felt a very sharp, unbearable pain deep within her spine. She cried out, "O my dear Lord, I cannot bear this pain any more. Help Me, O beloved Lord." In the distance she could see the Light once again. She could also see the Saint standing next to her, gently holding her hand. She could see her own birth, and all of a sudden she realized who she was and why she was here. The events of her life flashed past her, showing her all the accomplishments that she had endeavoured to achieve. She smiled with satisfaction. Suddenly she felt no more pain. The Light of Creation was right in front of her. The Light slowly engulfed her and finally absorbed her completely.

"Your Task is Complete," she heard the Voice of the Light say. At that point, Tara was no longer Tara. She had merged into the Light. She had achieved the purpose of her creation.

She left this world in peace. Her husband dearly held their little son as he bid farewell to his wife. His debt to her had been repaid and in the midst of his sorrow, he felt a special sense of peace and satisfaction.

A few years later, Tara's husband visited her grave one morning with their son. He read the inscription on her tombstone, which said, "She was born a mother and died a mother. She truly knew how to give to all. She is now like the Sun, who gives to all each day." Tara's husband pointed to the rising Sun and said to their son, "There rises your mother again. . . ."

Received on November 16, 1995.

NINE

𝒦ILIMANJARO:
A Parable of Life's Perspectives

The Voice of Inspiration says to the Herald, *"Look down the side of a mountain. What do you see? A mountain stands tall and strong and there is much to be learned by looking at its sides. Some sides are very steep with jagged edges. Others are gentle and smooth. Look at Mount Kilimanjaro. There is one way up that can be reached by walking and another by steep rock climbing. The events in a person's life are very comparable to the stories that are written along the sides of a mountain. There is much to be learned from them. . . ."*

On the slopes of Mount Kilimanjaro grew two tall trees. One tree's name was Miti and the other was called Evergreen. These trees had lived happily along the slopes of this majestic mountain for over a hundred years. Their position was unique because they stood almost halfway between the valley and the peak. They had seen many a courageous climber plod up towards the prized peak of Kilimanjaro.

One morning Miti said to Evergreen, "Did you watch that group of young boys heading up towards Gillman's Point this morning?"

Evergreen, the less observant of the two, said, "I heard them pass by us some time ago, but I caught just a glimpse of them in the distance around noon."

Miti replied, "When they passed by us, they were very energetic and talked about the climb up the mountain as if it were child's play. There is a boy in that group by the name of Alfred, who kept saying that this mountain was 'a piece of cake'! The guides cautioned him that there was still a long ways to go."

Evergreen laughed and commented, "I guess Alfred is in for an education, isn't he?"

Miti replied, "When you look downhill from where we are, you cannot tell that you have been climbing up the Great Kilimanjaro. It just looks like a simple incline of some gradually sloping hill. However, when you look uphill, it is a different story because you see the peak and the steep climb towards it. Therefore, Evergreen, it is purely a matter of perspective. Alfred kept looking behind and found everything to appear gentle and easy. He made the mistake of assuming that what lay ahead would be the same."

Evergreen commented sarcastically, "Maybe Alfred was unable to see clearly far ahead! Perhaps his eyesight was not good!"

Miti did not find this comment funny. "There was also that boy Victor, who kept saying that he would never be able to make it to the peak because the climb ahead looked too rough! Is it not strange that all the boys, who were climbing up the same mountain, saw their journey ahead so differently? One kept looking behind and thought that the journey was easy. Another kept looking ahead and thought that it was impossible. And I am sure that in some way they were both right!"

"I can see two reasons for their differences," Evergreen replied. "One is that each boy viewed the same slope from a different perspective. The other is that the mountain was probably playing tricks on their eyes, just like the great magician who plays with illusions!"

Miti then said, "The boy called Richard I thought rather wise. He said to his friends that the best way to reach the top was by not looking at the peak or the bottom, because both could be deceptive. Richard said that he only looked ahead in small and reachable measures, a hundred yards at a time. In this way, he was always calm and in control because he set his eyesight only on what was achievable."

Evergreen thought that Richard's approach was the best one. "I suppose for Richard's way to work, he must have a very clear idea of where he wants to end up. The risk with his approach is that if he climbs a hundred yards at a time, in a series of miscalculated directions, he could end up on the other side of the mountain, where only the specialists can climb with pickaxes!"

Miti agreed with Evergreen's observation. "If looking at the top or the bottom all the time is not the best way, then Richard's approach has to make the most sense. Of course Richard's steps, if not carefully directed, could take him around the mountain to the most dangerous side. But he looked like a smart boy who knew where he was headed."

Evergreen then commented, "Miti, since you and I cannot move up or down the mountain, we have the advantage of seeing things from one fixed vantage point. Therefore we are not fooled by the variations in the mountain slope."

Miti replied, "Actually, Evergreen, we are not necessarily in an advantaged position because we suffer from the limitations of having only a single perspective!"

"That is true," Evergreen agreed, "but I would argue that we are both well-balanced! Hence we are neither overconfident like Alfred nor scared like Victor!"

Miti replied, "We may not be overconfident or scared, but we are certainly limited by our singular perspective. We could not even argue over this issue because we know no different!"

"Why do we need to see more than one perspective, Miti?" asked Evergreen. "Aren't we just happy as we are? We get to see all these people going by us in pursuit of the peak, and then being only too happy to get down again! As they climb up, the mountain plays its tricks on their eyes by placing variations in slope, vegetation, rock types and many other things in the scene. The humans are a race that loves to be played with, and the mountain has its fun by placing illusions all around them!

"Once a climber said to her friend that the peak looked like it was touching the sky!

Another time I heard a climber on the way down tell his friend that the valley was so far away that he felt like he was entering a black hole—whatever that is! Miti, I am much happier with my single perspective, thank you very much! I do not need to have games of illusions played with my eyes by this master magician of a mountain!"

Miti, who was also a wise tree, said, "Evergreen, perhaps you are correct. You see, the two of us can survive with a single perspective, because we are not really going anywhere. For the human being, it is different. Can you imagine if Alfred only had the one perspective of ease and callousness? Or if all Victor could feel in life was terror and paranoia because that was his only perspective?"

Miti continued, "Richard is somewhat different because he uses many perspectives to arrive at his destination. He has the overall perspective of the peak and the valley. Then, he has the smaller perspectives of each hundred yards of his journey. Despite all his caution, Richard still runs the risk of straying away towards the perilous side of the mountain!"

"When a human climbs up a mountain, he or she strives to reach the peak," Evergreen replied. "On Mount Kilimanjaro, the journey can be easy or very difficult, depending on which side of the mountain one chooses to climb. Therefore the same destination can be reached by an easy or a very difficult path. To add to that, no matter what path one selects, the slope and surroundings vary with every few steps. Hence at some point along the journey a person may feel overconfident, like Alfred. Then, just a few steps ahead, the same person may feel terrified, like Victor. One certainty about the sides of this mountain is change!"

Evergreen continued, "If one breaks up the slope into reasonable measures, then the degree of change or variation is more manageable. Richard had the right idea. But was a hundred yards the right distance to base his view on? Maybe two hundred yards would have been better, or maybe fifty yards would have worked the best!"

Miti, quite amused with Evergreen's observations, replied, "You see, the poor human being has to get used to having lots of perspectives and being able to govern each perspective carefully if he or she is to reach their destination. I suppose a person's life is like the slope of the mountain, full of surprises and appearances that change every moment without warning! To make matters more interesting, one has to select the best side of the mountain to climb up or else one's progress can either be rapid or extremely slow. Yet despite all these options and routes, the destination is always the same! Evergreen, you are right—we are better off standing here as trees and enjoying the show!"

After the Herald had related the story of Miti and Evergreen, the Voice of Inspiration said, *"The life of a human being is an existence that is governed by great intelligence. The wise ones will recognize that every inch of this planet—and the Universe, for that matter—is different. Every observation carries a unique combination of perspectives. Each perspective is always correct for its beholder. Therefore much happiness can be found in life by accepting this simple fact. Most conflicts arise from intolerance towards other people's perspectives. Most successes are achieved through attitudes of confidence that have been regulated by wisdom that comes from being able to identify the potholes along the road. Misery and loss are often experienced by those who are paranoid about all that lies ahead of them."*

The Voice of Inspiration continued, *"The story of Miti, Evergreen and Mount Kilimanjaro offers food for thought. It provides a basis for people to think about their lives, their surroundings, their relationships, goals and objectives. The story also helps to shed light on how to recognize the sources of unhappiness that plague people's lives every day. . . ."*

Received on June 21, 1995.

TEN

THE ANCIENT CHURCH BELL: A MESSAGE FROM THE GREAT SOUL

The Herald sat under a tree in the village courtyard. He was surrounded by men, women and children who had travelled great distances to hear his extraordinary story—the story of his blessed encounter with the Great Soul.

"My dear friends," the Herald began, "I was out walking in the hills one dark night when I encountered an unusual sight. Suddenly in front of me there appeared the silhouette of an ancient church building with a tall steeple. I stopped and looked at this structure with great surprise because I knew of no buildings within miles of these remote hills! Everything around me was dark. There was no moon in the sky.

The only light I could see came from the stars. I was all alone and there was no living being around me.

As I looked at the steeple in the twilight, I felt a deep sense of loneliness. My eyes were fixed upon this ancient church. I had to ask myself, Where am I? Why am I here? In the depths of my loneliness I began to see this ancient church come slowly towards me. Most objects appear larger as they come closer— however, this church grew smaller and smaller until, as it stood next to me, the tip of the steeple was only as tall as my forehead! As the church touched me I began to feel a strong surge of power within me. The church slowly began to become a part of me. A few moments later, this ancient building had merged completely into me! I stood in the calm, still night all alone. There was no life around me and now there was also no church."

The Herald continued, "Suddenly I began to hear the distant ringing of a Bell, which seemed to be coming from the very depths of my Inner Self. Its sound was soft, gentle and soothing. I knew that this Bell was not being rung by a human being. I listened intently. The Bell began to repeat my name with warmth and energy. Its ringing seemed to be getting closer, but not necessarily louder. It began to talk to me with each and every ring. To my surprise, I clearly understood its language! The Bell delivered these special words to me:

"'O Herald, listen to the Truth and think no more, for all you must do is Listen! I am the Great Soul who came to this earth centuries ago to reveal to humanity the Truth about the Origin (Creator) and all Creation. I was placed in the womb of My mother, who delivered Me into this world of loneliness. As I grew up, there was joy all around Me, but I was always lonely. I was very different from everybody. This made Me lonely when I was amongst people. Yet when I was by Myself I was happy, for there was no more loneliness. I felt the closest to My Origin when I was all alone. When I set out on My Mission to teach the Truth to the people, I was rejected everywhere I went. The more they rejected Me, the stronger My will grew towards helping them. There were a precious few that listened to Me. And amongst them, too, I found no loyalty. Around Me there was emptiness. I taught them about the Truth. I rang out to them like the Bell of Truth which, O Herald, you hear now. But it was like ringing this wonderful Bell in a closed room. All it could do was to echo. The Truth could travel no further in this world!'

"The Great Soul continued, *'My Mission was to teach humanity about the Oneness of the Origin (Creator). I sought to teach them about morals, ethics and ways of living that would bring harmony within themselves, the Earth and their Origin. My Message to them was delivered in a form that was simple and easily understood. But I was ridiculed and rejected. Nevertheless I prayed for them during every moment of My life and thereafter. I stood up for the Truth and fought each day in the name of the Truth. I was tortured and humiliated. There was no part of My body that was spared from pain. Yet I carried on with nothing but Love in My heart until the time came when I returned Home, to the Light of My Origin again. After My death, a blessed vision of Me remained in the world as a reminder to all of what I had come to teach. A new religion started from My teachings, but it grew amidst conflict and disunity. My name was taken in vain to further the political ambitions of those who pretended to uphold My teachings. My words were misinterpreted to suit their purpose. After all, how can One Truth have thirty-three different versions?'*

"The Great Soul continued, *'Throughout the centuries, I have been there for whoever has remembered Me. I have even been there for those who have forgotten Me! This is true today and it will be so forever! I have spread Love and Light through My words, My sacrifices and My pain. After all these centuries, you can still see the signs of My Mission all over the world. I am saddened to see the growing numbers of people today who are disillusioned as they seek to follow My Teachings. This is because there is great confusion, fear and resentment which arises from the clouds of rituals, sectarianism and rigid institutional codes of conduct that have been imposed upon them. In today's age, people enjoy freedom of expression. They are free to exercise the broadest horizons of their Intellect. They cannot accept blindly the practice of a faith which is clouded with fear, restrictions, divisions and excessive material demands. It is My wish and prayer that humanity may seek out the Essence of My Teachings by setting aside notions and practices that do not appeal to their reason. This Essence can be discovered at a very personal level, in the absence of any prescribed rules or structures. Each man, woman and child may interpret whatever they will from My Teachings, for their interpretation comes from their Inner Selves, which is linked to the Truth. O Herald, tell the world about what I have said. For those who can learn from this Message, there is much to be gained. . . .'"*

As the people sat around the Herald, captivated with everything that they had heard, the Herald continued to relate his story.

"After the Great Soul had given me His message, the Bell began to slowly fade into the background. I felt a surge of power as I began to see the silhouette of the ancient church leave me. The church grew larger and larger as it moved away from me. There came a point when the steeple looked like it touched the sky, but it kept going higher and higher. In the twilight, I saw the silver reflection of the Bell at the top of the steeple. It kept swaying from side to side, ringing out the Truth for all to hear!

"My dear friends, think not about who the Great Soul was, rather reflect carefully on everything that He said. It does not matter what religion you belong to or what faith you believe in. Just seek the Essence behind your beliefs, because that is most important! Remember, your personal interpretation of the Essence will always be correct for you. Never doubt yourself! And if ever you are unsure of yourself, remember the guidance of the Great Soul. . . ."

Received on July 20, 1995.

ELEVEN

Fences:

The Parable of the Thai Farmer

There was once a young farmer in Thailand named Deng, who owned a large rice field. He produced the best harvests in the region and whoever tasted his rice always came back for more. Deng grew up in comfort and wealth because his father, Guam, owned large tracts of land in the region. Over time, this land had been divided into smaller plots, which were cultivated by the children of the family. In times of need, various parcels of this land were sold.

One evening after dinner, Deng and his father sat in their cozy living room in front of a warm log fire. As they stared into the blue-and-yellow flames, Guam said to his son, "Look at this fire. It started from a single log of wood. As this log burns, it shrinks and gives off light and heat. As the log disappears, don't you wonder where it went?"

Deng replied, "Father, the log converted itself into heat and light."

The wise Guam then said, "Where did this heat and light go? We cannot see where they went. Yet we can see that the log has shrunk."

Deng replied, "The log went from the visible to the invisible. As this occurred, we could experience the energies that were given off. But this experience only lasted for a few moments. Think how long the tree from which the wood came lived. Hundreds of years, maybe? Yet as we burned the log, it disappeared within minutes. What took hundreds of years to Be, took only a few moments to disappear."

Guam said to his son, "Let us think about where that tree came from. Before hundreds of years, what was it?"

"It was a seed, Father," Deng replied.

"What was it before it became a seed?" asked Guam.

Deng replied, "It was a fruit from a tree that lived before it."

Guam said to his son, "We can keep trying to trace the origin of the tree until we reach a point where we have to say that it came from the Unseen."

"That is true, Father," Deng replied. "After all those cycles of life of the tree, we finally burned the wood and now, we can see it no more! However, as it disappeared, we felt the heat and saw the light for a short while."

Guam then asked, "But aren't light and heat elements that made the tree grow in the first place?"

"Yes, they were the key elements that made the tree grow," Deng replied. "We could not see the tree consume light and heat. Yet we could see the wood that they helped produce. As the wood burned, these elements were revealed again for a brief period. Now they are gone and so is the wood!"

Guam said to his son, "Deng, I am seventy-eight years old. My life is coming to an end. I came from the Unseen, just like the tree. Then, as I grew, parts of me began to gradually die and disappear through each day of my life. Like the wood, I too have been slowly disappearing. But I ask myself very often whether I have generated any light and warmth for others to experience. At least, that is what the wood managed to do for us, didn't it? Tomorrow I will die and be buried and you will see me no more, just like the log that has burned away. I ask myself, What did I give to this world?"

Guam continued, "When my father died, he left me a large plot of land. I have divided up this land into smaller parcels for my children. I have also sold parcels of this beloved land, in exchange for money. Your brothers and sisters constantly fought over this land and now they have built fences to keep one another away. These fences have not only divided our land, they have divided my very own core, my very own heart! If your grandfather were alive today, he would grieve deeply to see our land divided up and fenced like this! At one time, it was our land. Now it has many individual owners, some of whom may be my children—but it is not our land any more. Tomorrow, my grandchildren will build more fences and the parcels of land will shrink further.

'Who knows, the land may never grow any rice again. Maybe each parcel will grow a different food. Maybe each parcel will be built up with houses and roads to form a town. Maybe this town will grow into a city. My dear Deng, you and your children will see this beloved land shrink each day before your very eyes. People may claim that it will be more valuable because of its diminishing supply. This may be true, but I don't believe it—I believe that it will have lost all of its true value! You see, my son, building fences is the worst thing one can ever do. The moment we build a fence, we begin to shrink from outside and from within. The more fences we build, the quicker we will disappear."

Deng, who had been listening intently to his father, then said, "When God created this Earth, it had no boundaries. Human beings built fences which formed countries. As a civilization, we have continued to shrink from within throughout this cycle. We started as one family and now we have become hundreds of countries. We not only divide our land, we divert and stop rivers from flowing freely, to capture their water. Some countries carelessly pollute their air, setting up consequences in other countries. You see, Father, what happened to our farm has indeed happened to the entire world from the time of its creation."

"That is correct, my son," Guam replied. "You see, what took a seed hundreds of years to grow into a tree was burned so rapidly right in front of our eyes. We felt the heat and saw the light for a precious few moments. In the same way, what took our family generations to build—our farm—has shrunk, with fences erected all over it in one generation! As it shrank, no light or heat was felt. All that was experienced was greed, selfishness and anguish.

Soon it will all be over. We will ask ourselves, What did we achieve? The entire world, as it keeps dividing itself, will ask the question, What did we achieve?

"I do not know the answers to these questions. But I do know that if the tree were to ask me what it had achieved, I could certainly say to it, 'You have lit our hearts and warmed our homes.' I know that the tree would reply, 'Then you must learn from Me.' But, my dear son, I am seventy-eight years old! Even if I tried to learn from the tree, I have no time left to do much about it."

Deng looked into his father's eyes and said, "At least you have taught me to do something about it. I am forty years old and I do have time on my side. Thanks to you, my beloved Father! By teaching me all the virtues of life you have become my anchor, my tree, who has warmed my life and lit up my mind and soul. Therefore, my beloved Father, at seventy-eight, you are not old at all. In my heart, you will live forever!"

Received on February 11, 1996.

TWELVE

THE *Eternal Pool*:
THE PARABLE OF EBRAHIM AND SARAH

In the middle of a dense forest lived two children by the name of Ebrahim and Sarah. They had no parents, but indeed, they were not orphans! They lived among the shelter of the trees and ate the foods that were provided to them by the forest.

In spite of the fact that they had no human parents, they were sustained in every way by the love and purity of the trees, flowers and all the creatures in the forest. Each time they craved food there was fruit available that would satisfy them. Each time they were unwell a healing herb was available. Each time they were thirsty, water of the pure, crystal-clear river would quench their thirst. All that they needed to learn was taught to them through the ways of the trees, flowers, rivers and creatures of the forest.

In the night they learned about that which could not be seen, and in the day they learned about that which could be seen. At the exact line that divides day from night, which is at dawn and at dusk, they learned about that which could not be seen either in the day or in the night. This was the time for them to see "themselves", to reflect and gain Knowledge of everything.

Thus Ebrahim and Sarah remained innocent. Their minds were "open" to pure Knowledge. Their hearts were "open" to pure Love. They gave as freely as they took, for they were surrounded with abundance. Their existence was pure. They were never lonely because they were a pair; they had each other and they had their own individual selves. Such is the way that life was for Ebrahim and Sarah.

One morning as they walked in the forest they came to a group of seven very old, tall trees, whose roots grew under and above the ground. The trees grew in a circle and their roots twined into one another. Ebrahim and Sarah stopped and looked at them in awe. How beautiful they were! The trees had an aura that bore a deep sense of wisdom. As the children looked up, they could see that the seven trees touched the skies! They were of unending height!

Ebrahim and Sarah stepped closer to the centre of the circle. In the very middle gushed a fountain of clear, pure water. The fountain had a stem in its centre and the water fell from the top of this stem in the form of a perfect circle. It was like looking at a perfect crystal mushroom. Curious as they were, the children sought to take a drink from this fountain. They were surprised to find that the fountain was not really water. It did not even wet their hands! They looked at the bottom of the fountain stem and it seemed like this magical water was coming from an opening deep, deep within the earth. The opening went as far under the ground as the seven trees rose toward the sky. Sarah, disappointed that she could not get a drink from this fountain, said to Ebrahim, "This water is strange but unkind. I am thirsty and it did not give me what I wanted."

Ebrahim replied, "Sarah, this is not water! Whatever this fountain is, it is very special. It has roots that go deep into the earth and it is protected by trees that touch the sky! I have never seen anything like this before!"

THE ETERNAL POOL: THE PARABLE OF EBRAHIM AND SARAH

Ebrahim and Sarah heard the Voice of Inspiration speak to them from within the fountain. This was the Voice that taught them about the "Unseen" at dusk and dawn each day. The Voice said to them, *"Children, you have found the Eternal Pool. This Pool has no beginning and no end. It is of the forest and it is not of the forest. It is of this world and it is not of this world. Whilst it looks like water, it is not water. But see! Look carefully—it Flows! It Flows Continuously. It is the Eternal Pool. From this Pool, you can draw all that you need, anything and everything! You cannot touch or feel this Pool but it can provide you with Everything. It even Flows within you at all times, but you are not aware of it. Remember though, it must always Flow. It can never become stagnant. Those that are part of its Flow will receive more and more. Those that try to stop its Flow will lose everything. They will be left with nothing. This, Ebrahim and Sarah, is the Law of the Eternal Pool. You are being shown this Pool for you are now ready to receive your offspring. You will have children that are little forms of you. They will grow up and have children of their own. Thus there will be many, many, many of you! There will be so many of you that the forest will have to keep stretching itself each day to look after you. But remember that you and your children will receive all your needs from this Pool. As you receive you must give, for this Pool must always Flow; its cycle must always be complete. If you stop giving, then you will be stopping its Flow and that would cut you out from everything."*

Ebrahim and Sarah asked, "But how could one ever stop giving? That is just not the way of the forest."

The Voice replied, *"Indeed, you cannot imagine what it is like not to give, because you have been nurtured by a Balance in the forest. You have been nurtured by Nature. Giving is an essence of Nature. Yet, as you have children, they may cause the forest to change, which may cause the Balance to break. When this happens, everything will change. But remember, Ebrahim and Sarah, inscribe in the hearts of your children the Law of the Eternal Pool. Inscribe in their hearts that everything must Flow through them at all times. Inscribe in their hearts that each time they give, no matter how little or how much, they are keeping the Flow of the Eternal Pool going. Inscribe in their hearts that no matter how much they receive from the Eternal Pool, they must always give part of it back. In this way the cycle will always be complete. If they were to receive ten fruits, they should give back at least one fruit, for the Flow must always prevail."*

THE ETERNAL POOL: THE PARABLE OF EBRAHIM AND SARAH

Ebrahim and Sarah asked together, "How can our children give back to the Pool?"

The Voice replied, *"By giving to each other, by helping those in need, by caring for the Earth and all its creatures, by caring for the sky and all its creatures, by caring for the water and all its creatures. Remember, the Eternal Pool flows through all Creation. They may draw from it all they need, for it is limitless. But they must obey the Law of Flow. Teach them that they must give back at least one fruit from every ten fruits they receive. Those that do not do this will fall by the wayside, for their Balance will be broken. The Pool will give you all wealth, love, happiness, skills and everything else that you need. Remember that it is Eternal and it is Limitless. Look at these seven trees. They take and they give! Look at them—do they not touch the sky? Well, Ebrahim and Sarah, so can you!"*

The two beautiful children had learned much from the Eternal Pool. As they walked away, they thought about the seven tall trees. They thought about their tightly intertwined roots, which were both Seen and Unseen. Their stems, which could be Seen so clearly, touched the sky. There were so many symbols that were embodied in these seven trees. Ebrahim and Sarah reflected upon the Eternal Pool. They now understood how nature provided for all their needs. They had been a part of the Flow of this Pool each and every day of their lives. Now they were to have their offspring. This was to be a new experience. For the first time ever, they were faced with the prospect of thinking about the Future. . . .

Received on February 21, 1996.

THIRTEEN

THE *I*NSTRUMENTS OF *L*IFE: A PARABLE OF REAL PEOPLE

The Voice of Inspiration says to the Herald, *"Speak about Instruments. What is their role? How do they affect the lives of human beings and, for that matter, all of Creation? People see and experience Instruments daily, in many, many forms, but seldom are they recognized. Relate the parable of the Instruments, for there are useful lessons for those that are seeking happiness and fulfilment in their lives."*

In the early evening in a small village in Africa, tribesmen hurried to bring their cattle from the grazing plains back into the village compound, where they would be safe for the night. The womenfolk lit the daily fire in the centre of the compound as the cool wind began to turn chilly. Mothers stirred their black pots of millie meal and gravy while their little ones patiently watched. This was a wonderful sight. It was almost as if the setting of the Sun had brought all creatures closer and closer into this village, so that they might be fed and enjoy shelter for the night.

By contrast, at midday the village compound lay almost deserted. The men were all out herding the cattle, hunting and tilling the fields. The women fetched water and firewood, and plucked leaves and herbs for the evening dinner. Precious few remained at the village at the midday hour. What a change in the evening when everyone and everything came together.

As all these wonderful events occurred, the two Angels, Cyrus and Luminus, watched with amusement and satisfaction. Cyrus said to Luminus, "Look how hard these people have worked throughout the day to care for themselves, their families, children, land and cattle! Now they will all come together for a precious few hours to share their meal, warm themselves by their fires and rest for the night.

Tomorrow the Sun will rise and so will start again their work of the day! What is being achieved by these people each day? They are all serving one another, their land, their herds and their surroundings. All they do throughout their day is to give. Whatever they receive is shared in the evening in an atmosphere of peace, love and unity."

The Angel Luminus replied, "These people are Instruments. They are in harmony. Hence their music is sweet and although their lives are tough, they enjoy a special joy with the passage of each day. These people, my dear Cyrus, are Instruments."

At that moment the two Angels turned around and decided to take a look at what was happening in New York City. What a dramatic difference! They watched the busy people running around, the yellow cabs buzzing away like bees. Every second, people exchanged green dollar bills with one another; some argued, some laughed, some cried and some just watched! Then the Angels entered the New York Stock Exchange building. Luminus, who loved action, decided to take a peek at the trading floor. People shouted and ran, exchanging tickets and looking at screens. Each moment someone's fortune was made while another's was ruined. Numbers raged across screens as shares, bonds, futures and options traded furiously.

Cyrus said to Luminus, "Let's get out of here, for this scene is truly unreal! Look at these people! They are trading on things that do not even exist! And fortunes are being made and lost every minute! Where is the life here? Where is the reality here?"

Luminus, who was enjoying the action, said, "Come on, Cyrus, why not take a few moments and watch this circus with me! There are acrobats here that can never be found anywhere in the world! There are magicians here that create something from nothing! And there are the sheep who lose everything for nothing! It is a fun show and it costs us nothing to watch."

Cyrus, not impressed with all this, reluctantly agreed to stay back and watch the scene. Then the bell rang and it was all over. The screen showed the Dow Jones at 4210, up 30 points on the day. Everyone began to leave and within minutes the place was more deserted than a graveyard. The show was over.

Luminus said to Cyrus, "After all that frenzy, with winners and losers and blazing telephones and screens, the Dow Jones is up thirty points! What does that mean? And why have 4210 and not 49,999? What has really been achieved here? Now there are the sweepers cleaning the floors of this quiet graveyard, which will burst out again in the morning and paper will fly all over again for the Dow to close *down* 28 points tomorrow! If you want to find great illusions on this Earth, here is the place to look! Have no fear, my dear Cyrus. If you can't find an illusion, these little men will create one for you and then they will all bet on whether your new illusion will grow or shrink! They'll give it a few points either way!"

The Angels left the Stock Exchange building and looked over the city. There were people rushing in all directions. Cyrus asked Luminus, "Did you see any Instruments here today?"

Luminus quietly replied, "A few, a precious few. But they were around." As they spoke, on the other side of the world the fire in the African village compound had faded to a glow. Cyrus said to Luminus, "At each moment in time, there is such a sharp contrast in the lives of people in this world."

Then the Angels decided to take a look at India. They watched the activities taking place in and around the store of a Mr. Ramchand in Bombay. A mother walked in with her daughter to buy their rations for the day. As they picked up their provisions, the mother asked Mr.

Ramchand why the price of rice had increased 20 percent that day.

"We have a shortage," said the storekeeper. "Because of that, you have to pay more."

Luminus and Cyrus looked at each other and said, "Nonsense! His stores are full!"

Mr. Ramchand took more money from the mother and daughter on the false pretext of a rice shortage in the city. Of course they had no choice, so they paid the higher price. In this way, Mr. Ramchand collected record profits for the day by deceiving his poor customers.

Luminus said to Cyrus, "This man would do very well at the New York Stock Exchange! The only difference is that he has sold real rice in exchange for real money. I suppose we can say that the Ramchand Index has closed up twenty points today. The Ramchand Index is now at 2010!"

Cyrus chuckled and replied, "Well, I like the number 3019—so let us say that the Ramchand Index is at 3019!"

The Angels laughed and took their leave. As they looked over the city of Bombay, they saw the mother and daughter heading home. The Angels stopped to watch what was happening. The mother knocked at the door of a poor old sick lady and then quietly stepped into the hut.

She took a portion of the rice that she had bought from Mr. Ramchand and placed it in a saucepan in the kitchen. The old lady said to the mother in a weak voice, "Bless you, my child. What would I have ever done without you? May God send Angels like you to bring hope to the homes of many, many other destitutes like me."

The mother replied, "You are not destitute, my dear friend, for God takes care of all of us." After feeding the old lady, the mother and daughter headed off towards their own home. On the way they made two additional stops in order to share their provisions with the needy.

Luminus said to Cyrus, "If only Mr. Ramchand could see what he has done by overcharging this beautiful Angel! She and her daughter will barely have anything left for dinner. But of course, the few grains that they eat will fill them and give them greater satisfaction than all the rice in the world ever could."

Cyrus replied, "They are Instruments. What they have done is Real. They have worked hard and shared with others whatever little they could. They are Instruments."

The Angels then turned towards London and the laboratory of Professor Mark Sheriden. After years of research, the professor had finally made a breakthrough in finding a cure for cancer! There was celebration and jubilation as the laboratory staff shared their excitement with the professor. "You will be a very rich man, Professor," said Lisa, the laboratory technician.

"It may be so, but that is not important," replied the professor. "My reward will come from seeing the number of lives saved from our work. We will have eliminated many a tear, my dear Lisa. That is important."

Then John, the laboratory manager, said to the professor, "We must patent this cure immediately before our ideas are stolen."

"Who said that it was our idea?" the professor replied. "All we did was discover this cure through Inspiration. This cure is to be shared and not hoarded for profit."

Luminus said to Cyrus, "It's a good job Professor Mark does not know Mr. Ramchand!"

The laboratory manager then said, "I realize your point, Professor, but we live in a day and age where we must protect ourselves."

The professor replied, "You are right, John. We need this protection to share our discovery properly and fairly with others."

Just then the phone rang and it was George, the professor's son, who was a stockbroker with Merrill Lynch in New York. The professor said to George, "Son, all the money that you have invested in the laboratory has paid off—we have found the cure for cancer!"

George, who had shared in his father's vision, said, "Well done, Dad—we've made it! Now you can fulfil what you have always dreamed of doing. You can now help eliminate pain and suffering. For my part, Dad, I have only helped in a small way."

The professor said, "Son, you provided all the nourishment for the seed of my research to germinate and grow. Without your funding we could never have made it."

George quietly replied, "We will now go forward and raise more money in the stock market to help you to correctly implement the cure for cancer in the exact manner that you had dreamed of, Dad. Well, congratulations and thanks to God!"

Luminus said to Cyrus, "Remember at the New York Stock Exchange I told you that I saw some Instruments? Well, George happened to be one of them. He was present on the trading floor at the time. In the midst of the stock-market illusion, he created something real by being the financier for a cure that will positively impact the lives of millions." Both Angels said together, "George and his father are Instruments."

In a single day, the Angels saw Instruments at work throughout the world, from Africa to America to India and England. They smiled as they looked down upon the Earth and said, "Instruments are the Tools that keep the world turning. . . ."

Received on August 24, 1995.

FOURTEEN

THE ℬEDOUIN:
A PARABLE OF THE DESERT

The Herald is told by the Voice of Inspiration: *"Write about 'Authority.' In the world that is dominated by all aspects of the material, what is the true meaning of the word 'Authority'? In the Inner Self of each being has been instilled a sense of 'Will.' This sense was bestowed for a greater purpose than what it is applied towards today. 'Authority' is a term that is responsible for a lot of the grief, confusion and disillusionment that is felt by such a large proportion of humanity. Write about what Authority really ought to be. Explain how it can be applied towards the positive enhancement of the application of the Will.*

The Herald relates the following parable, which beautifully describes the concepts of "Authority", "Will" and "Self Application" as they may be applied in our daily lives.

There was once a Bedouin who travelled through the deserts of Arabia on his camel. He was a nomad and had no real place that he could call home. On this particular day he walked in the blazing midday sun towards the Oasis, which he knew lay somewhere between his current position and his ultimate destination in the desert. He stopped for a little break and pulled out his gourd of water to quench the burning thirst that raged in his throat. The water was warm, and while it quenched his thirst, it did not leave him fully satisfied. His mind flashed to the Oasis, where a cool drink of water awaited him from the gourd that sat in the shade of the date palms. Having completed his drink, he started to walk again.

Thirty minutes later his throat began to burn again and he stopped once more to take a drink. He thought to himself: If I stop for a drink this often, I will never get to my destination; from here on, I will not stop any more. However, thirty minutes later his throat was on fire again! He fought back the urge to drink the warm water in his gourd. He fought and fought, until an hour later he succumbed to his thirst. He drank from the gourd.

The thirst had "Authority" over him and he had to succumb to it. But this was an assertion of Authority that was tailored to save him and protect him from the blazing desert heat. The Authority was so powerful that it overcame his inner Will to resist it. My dear friends, here is an example of "Authority" as it is applied in a natural sense to protect the poor Bedouin. He did not enjoy his drink because it was warm and tasteless. Yet he needed it to survive. Therefore, the thirst exercised its Authority over him. Remember, the Bedouin had an inner Will but the Authority of the thirst was too great for the Will to resist. This is an example of the application and interaction of Authority and Will within a natural context.

By early evening the Bedouin saw the Oasis in the distance—his heart leapt with joy. As he came closer to it he saw tents, and children playing in a central enclosure. A few moments ago, everything was lifeless. Now all of sudden he was in the middle of life itself!

A little boy came running towards him, holding out a small, tender hand in greeting towards the Bedouin. They shook hands like friends and the boy said to the Bedouin, "Welcome to our home, O traveller. Come rest your feet and dine with us, for it would be our honour to have you as our guest."

The Bedouin was taken aback by the warmth and the kind gesture of the eight-year-old. "I thank you, O little one—but don't you think you should ask your parents if it is all right for me to dine with you?"

"No, indeed not, O dear traveller!" little Imran replied. "My parents are servants of the Origin, who provides for all of us, and in whose name we share what has been bestowed upon us with others."

The Bedouin replied, "But to be honest with you, my dear little friend, it is your parents that have the Authority to invite me, is it not?"

The child replied, "No, indeed it is not, for the Origin has bestowed upon us all the Authority to share the bounty with whomever we will!"

The Bedouin said, "Then, in God's name, I accept your invitation! My Will is yours!"

My dear friends, here is an example of Authority being exercised out of love, giving and sharing. The Will accepts this Authority in that very spirit.

THE BEDOUIN: A PARABLE OF THE DESERT

The Bedouin enjoyed the lovely dinner that was offered to him by Imran's family. After his meal, he called Imran and said, "Can you get me a drink of cool water, Imran?"

The little boy's eyes were sleepy. He replied, "The gourd is over there under the date palm. I bid you to get it yourself, for I am falling asleep."

The Bedouin felt restless and impatient. He raised his voice in frustration and said, "Child, when I tell you to do something, you do it!"

Poor little Imran was startled and got up to run over to the gourd and fetch the drink. Just then, his Will stopped him. He said, "By what Authority do you order me, O traveller?"

The Bedouin replied, "I am older than you, and by virtue of my age I have Authority over you!"

To this Imran replied, "You may believe that you have Authority over me, but my Will does not accept!"

The Bedouin pulled out his stick and said, "Then I will have to use the Authority of this stick to make you move!"

Little Imran ran over and brought him the water and said, "I bring this to you out of Fear, and not by my Will."

My dear friends, the true joy and love in any act is where the Authority and the Will are in harmony. Authority can only come from natural sources. The Bedouin's Authority came from a false use of force that prompted Fear and not free acceptance by the Will! He or she who has true Authority never needs to exercise it, for the Will of the other always follows.

This is how the concept of Respect comes to bear. Those that do not possess Authority try to imagine and act as if they have it. However, in such cases, all they draw upon is Fear and not harmony of the Will. Some people will do anything for others out of their own free Will because of Respect that has been cultivated within them. The recipient of such actions has true Authority, for there is harmony in every ensuing action. Authority and Will are like two poles of a magnet—they must attract! The introduction of Fear destroys this harmony.

In the material world, people exercise a perceived Authority over others by virtue of their wealth, status and power. This, my dear friends, is not Authority—it is blackmail! If we truly want to enjoy a harmonious relationship with our loved ones and all those around us, we must remember that the exercise of Authority and attraction of a response by Will is essential. People will then learn to love and Respect us, as we will them. This is a golden key to harmonious relationships—two simple words: Authority and Will.

Received on June 15, 1995.

FIFTEEN

THE SPINNING GLOBE:
A PARABLE OF THE CYCLE OF LIFE

The Voice of Inspiration says to the Herald, *"The Earth is oval in shape. It spins around its axis and travels through the solar system in an appointed fashion. Look at the globe. At its tips lie the coldest of places, the Arctic and the Antarctic Circles. At its centre lies the Equator, where one can find the hottest of places. These unique characteristics of the Earth represent some important parallels with the life cycle of a human being. Write about the experience of Rahim, the scientist, to explain these parallels more clearly."*

THE SPINNING GLOBE: A PARABLE OF THE CYCLE OF LIFE

It was 6:00 p.m. in Singapore. Rahim, a successful research scientist involved with numerous projects around the world, decided to call his parents in North America to say hello. He had not spoken to them for several weeks. Rahim was born and brought up in Pakistan, in a city called Lahore. He was the youngest of three children.

At the early age of 16, Rahim's parents sent him to the United Kingdom for higher education. He became a scientist and his career took him to North America. He set up his own research laboratories there; Rahim had dreams of developing technologies in the health-care field that would help prevent needless death and suffering in the developing world. These goals took Rahim to many corners of the world. He became a modern-day nomad who lived in the international skies. However, he called his wife and children every day, no matter where he was in the world. He also kept in regular contact with his parents, who had moved from Pakistan now and lived in North America.

Rahim picked up the telephone in his hotel room in Singapore and dialled the telephone number of his parents. As he waited for the call to go through, his mind flashed back to when he was a little child. He loved it when his father carried him on his shoulders and ran around the garden. He remembered his father as being a very energetic, youthful man. Yet now, at the other end of the line, was an elderly man who spoke softly and slowly. Rahim was delighted to talk to his father, but in his heart Rahim knew that his hero was losing strength and vigour as each day went by.

In contrast, Rahim was always energized when he called his wife and children. He marvelled at how his two sons and two daughters were growing up to become such warm, compassionate and intelligent people. Their level of energy kept increasing as each day went by. Every time he looked at his children, he could see "the future." Yet each time he spoke to his parents, his mind immediately flashed to "the past." Why was this so? he wondered.

It was during this telephone conversation with his father that the coin dropped! As soon as he hung up the receiver, he saw a beautiful image of a globe spinning around in front of him. It rotated gracefully in space. Its northern tip was beautiful, pristine and white. It was very cold, but Rahim sensed a purity in this North Pole. It was also very still. Very few human beings or creatures moved around—everything was calm and still. The ocean was covered with glaciers. Rahim thought to himself, This is wonderful; I could live here forever if only it were not so cold! Then he

The Spinning Globe: A Parable of the Cycle of Life

smiled and thought, But if it were warmer there would be no ice and no such beauty! Neither would it be so calm and still. While the North Pole was most attractive to Rahim, it was not perfect because of the chilling cold.

Then his eyes began to work their way downwards from the North Pole. Everything began to move faster as he looked southwards. The level of motion kept increasing. Everything was bursting with life. The colours of the forests and trees were absolutely enchanting. But everything was getting busier and busier; the energy level was extremely high. As he looked below the Tropic of Cancer, he noticed the level of motion continuing to increase. Then as his eyes began to focus on the Equator, he noticed that the energy levels were at a peak. This was the hottest part of the globe. Nothing was still any more; everything was in a constant state of motion. He thought: This place is too hot for me; there is a lot of action out here, but it is way too hot!

As Rahim looked below the Equator, he noticed that the trend had begun to reverse. As the heat dropped, so did the level of motion. The Tropic of Capricorn mirrored what he had seen at the Tropic of Cancer. Then he found himself looking at the South Pole, which was once again calm, pure and beautiful. But it was very, very cold.

The globe continued to spin in front of Rahim's eyes. The North Pole gave him a sense of peace and calmness, as did the South Pole. It was the lack of motion that he loved the most. Yet the cold made him feel like he did not belong there. At the Equator, everything moved around so fast that he could not see any calmness. He did not want to be there, either! Then he asked himself the question: If the North Pole and South Pole could be made warmer while maintaining their beauty and calmness, would it not be perfect? However, he knew that once these places became warmer, the very things that made them beautiful would disappear!

He asked himself, What would happen if the Equator were to cool down? If so, could the North and South Poles survive? Throughout this beautiful spinning globe, everything was somehow in balance. Whatever it was that made a given point imperfect on the globe was exactly what was required to make another point perfect. For example, the heat of the Equator, if transferred to the North Pole, would make things more desirable there. Or the cold from the North Pole, if carried down to the Equator, would make things more bearable there. Rahim asked himself, Could one exchange these elements of imperfection to create perfection? Would it be practical?

Then he thought of his father again. He remembered the energy and vigour of his father in days gone by. Now things had changed and the very same man had slowed down so much. Rahim wondered, Where would my father be in the context of this spinning globe? Would he be at the Equator? Of course not! He probably represents the South Pole. I see in him an immense beauty that stems from his wisdom and knowledge. He is also very calm and peaceful. But he is physically very slow, which is synonymous with the cold in the Antarctic. When I was a child, I remember my father being full of energy. He was probably at the Equator then. He was a lot of fun! Yet he also tended to be very brash, as my mother can vividly recall. Sometimes he was impossible to be with! My first memories of my father started at this point. Hence each time I look at him, I tend to drift from the South Pole up to the Equator. This is why the thought of my father always takes me into the past.

Then Rahim thought of his children. When they were born there was calmness around them. Since they could not move and run around, they were in a state of stillness. They were the most beautiful and precious little beings. They were innocent and pure. The very best moments of Rahim's life were when he watched the births of his children. He asked himself, Where were they on the globe at that time? They must have been like the North Pole! As they grew older, they began to move towards the Equator. They are not yet at the Equator, thank God!

As he watched the globe spinning steadily, Rahim realized that all the phases of life were clearly represented here. The purity, peace and beauty of the North Pole marked the start of life. The Equator marked its peak and the South Pole marked its end. The imperfection of the South Pole was the slowness caused by age. Yet this very age carried wisdom and calmness. If this wisdom were carried back to the Equator, so much more could be achieved.

Rahim could see the flow of life as his eyes worked their way from the North Pole to the South Pole. He realized how much his parents had to offer to him while he was at the Equator. Of course, as a baby, they provided for his basic necessities. Yet today, at his peak, there was so much wisdom and counsel that he could draw from them. They could help bring perfection to his imperfect, hot Equator!

Then Rahim began to reflect on his children. Portrayed by the North Pole, his children represented a solid foundation. It was a foundation based on purity, innocence and calmness. Rahim could see much of himself in his children. If life were comparable to the construction of a building, they represented the pillars that gave him strength. Yet in his parents he saw the completed building itself. In this intricate picture, he lay somewhere in between!

Rahim recognized that if he could bring to the Equator the purity, beauty and honesty from the North Pole and combine it with the wisdom and knowledge from the South Pole, he could bring himself closer to perfection.

Rahim said to himself, The spinning globe has shown me the entire flow of life. It spins at all times at a constant speed. This is synonymous with life itself! The North and South Poles keep the globe together and united. These are fundamental aspects of a true Family. They are essential for my peaceful existence. The Equator has the largest area and circumference. This is where my horizons are at their broadest levels. Therefore I must aim to achieve my very best at the Equator, by drawing upon the strength and wisdom that come from the North and South Poles. There are indeed many lessons for me to draw from the spinning globe. I must always reflect and meditate upon it!

A year later Rahim's father passed away. Three years later his mother also passed away. However, all that he had learned from his parents ensured that the South Pole was always

alive for him. He knew that he too was headed for this Pole with peace, calmness and dignity. The spinning globe had shown him a beautiful definition of Family. It had enriched his life considerably. He watched his children grow older and realized that he still had so much to give them. But did they realize how much more they could gain from him? He prayed that the spinning globe would appear to them someday.
. . .

Received on November 14, 1995.

SIXTEEN

Drawing Upon the Powers of Nature: the Parable of the Himalayan Shepherd

There was once a shepherd who lived in the valleys of the great Himalayan Mountains. His name was Zaheeb, and his life was one of great simplicity. He had never married. Very early each day he would take his flock of sheep out into the fields to graze. Then he would sit on his favourite rock in the valley and watch his sheep graze. Around noon hour he would feed on the dried foods that he carried with him. At midafternoon each day he would take his sheep to the river, where they could get their drink of pure water. He loved to sit at the bank of the river and watch the water flow with great speed, clarity and decisiveness. His eyes would glance upward towards the snow-capped peaks, where he knew these rivers originated.

Towards sunset he would walk his sheep back to his little farm, where they would be allowed to wander around within a small fenced area that he had prepared for them. Zaheeb had no family and he lived by himself. At the end of a day of caring for his sheep he would spend some time cooking, eating and completing his chores. After supper, he loved to sit by the fire outside his hut and look out at the stars. He had a name for each star in the sky. Just as he knew all his sheep, he also knew all the stars that he could see—as well as all the rocks in the river and all the trees in the field. Zaheeb had absorbed a great deal from his surroundings. He spoke to no other human for days and months on end. Yet he was content and happy.

One day as he sat in the field watching his sheep, he spotted a tall man with a grey beard walking towards him. This man was probably sixty years old. He wore a brown cape and carried a staff; with its help he walked steadily across the fields. As the man drew closer, Zaheeb stared more intently at him. There was something unusual about him, but Zaheeb could not quite tell what it was.

"Peace be upon you, O Shepherd," the man said in greeting to Zaheeb.

"Peace be upon You," Zaheeb replied. The man quietly walked over and sat down next to Zaheeb on the rock.

"What brings you to these fields, O friend?" asked Zaheeb.

The man replied, "I am looking for a man with great Knowledge and wisdom. I am told he lives in this valley."

Zaheeb replied, "I do not know of such a person and I am one of the very few people that live in this valley. There is no wise, learned man that I know of, O dear friend. You may have come to the wrong place."

The stranger looked at Zaheeb and said, "The man I seek does certainly reside here. He is full of Knowledge and wisdom. I have come here to seek answers to certain questions from him."

Zaheeb opened his little lunch pack and invited the man to share his meal. As they ate, a silence fell upon them. It was a strange silence, but for Zaheeb, silence was the main language he knew. Then the stranger looked at Zaheeb and began to speak.

"There was once a child born in a village, high up on this mountain. His father was a merchant who travelled from mountain to mountain in order to trade with the other villages. His mother, who cared very deeply for her little boy, stayed at home. She took him with her everywhere she went. They had some sheep, which the mother also looked after. This boy saw very little of his father. In fact, one day when he was only two years old, his father left on a journey and never returned.

"His mother waited at the cliff on the side of the mountain each day in the hope that her husband would return that day. Each day as the sun set, without fail she stood at the same spot and looked out into the distance. As darkness fell, she returned to their hut. The little boy also looked out for his father each day. He was very young, but he knew that one day he would see the mule in the distance, carrying his father home. But this did not happen.

"One day when he was five years old, he sat with his mother at the river while she brought the sheep for a drink. Suddenly, one of the sheep fell into a deep stream of fast-flowing water in the river. His mother rushed to rescue the sheep and in the process, she too got carried away by the river. The little boy did all he could to save his mother, but in a few moments she was gone. . . . He was now all alone.

Drawing Upon the Powers of Nature: the Parable of the Himalayan Shepherd

"After the loss of his mother, the boy stopped looking out for his father each day. Strangely, he thought of his father as having been grouped with his mother and when she was gone, he no longer searched for the man he had dutifully sought each day. This little boy grew up caring for his sheep. He spoke to no one. Yet he is the most learned, wisest man in this region. I have travelled far and to many different lands in search of this man. I was guided to this valley in my search."

Zaheeb looked at the stranger and asked, "What is it that guided you to this very valley? How could you be so sure to find the man that you seek here?"

The stranger replied, "Each night I look at the stars and there is one star in particular that always points toward where this man is. Each river I walk past sings his praises in the sounds of the water. Each time the Sun rises and sets, I read in it the signs that guide me to this man. So here I am; I know that my search is over. I have found the man I seek."

"I am but a simple shepherd who lives by himself," Zaheeb replied. "I have not been with people. I am not a learned man. All I am is a part of this valley, this mountain, this river and these fields. I spend my days caring for my sheep and looking at all the beautiful things around me. I see little creatures take birth and die in these fields each day. At night I look at the stars and read the stories that they tell. I am no man of Knowledge, nor am I so wise, for all I know about is the very simple things."

The stranger smiled and put his arms around Zaheeb and said, "Indeed, I was told that this is what the wise man would say when I found him!"

Zaheeb smiled at the stranger and said, "My name is Zaheeb; I am the shepherd of this valley. You have travelled so far to find me. I welcome you as my brother and my guest. What is it that you seek from me?"

The stranger looked at Zaheeb and asked, "When you are out in the fields and there is a thunderstorm that is raging in the skies, what do you do?"

Zaheeb replied, "Of course, I go to my shelter."

The other man then said, "No, there is something else that you do. What is it?"

Zaheeb looked into the eyes of his visitor and realized that this man knew a lot about him. He then said, "If the thunder does not die down, I look into the sky and pull the thunderclouds apart. As they become smaller clouds, they blow away quickly and the thunder is over. There is nothing unusual about that, is there?"

The older man replied, "Of course not—you just stop the thunderstorm as you will!"

Zaheeb smiled and said, "It is just a little understanding that I have with the clouds. So, what else can I tell you about?"

The older man then asked, "You are all alone and you do not receive any supplies for your home. Tell me, for example, how do you light your fire each evening?"

Zaheeb replied, "I do not know what supplies you talk about. Each day, at sunset, I look into the Sun and draw its rays into the logs that I have set out. This is how I light my fire. There is nothing special about it."

The visitor then asked, "How do you draw in the Sun's rays? I mean, the Sun is so hot, it could burn you and everything around here!"

Zaheeb smiled and said, "The Sun is not hot. The Sun is like a tree that grows a hundred different types of fruit. Whatever fruit you seek, it will give to you. It is very simple: I look at this beautiful Sun each day and I ask for a ray to light my fire. It really is very simple."

The visitor was most impressed. He then said, "Zaheeb, you live all by yourself. When you become ill, how do you get cured? You do not receive any medicines or supplies here. How do you heal yourself when you are hurt?"

Zaheeb looked up at the sky and then at the other man. He did that three times and then said, "You see, whenever I am unwell or I have hurt myself, I look at my body and I ask it to heal. It's very simple."

The old man said, "What do you mean when you say that you look at your body? You have no mirrors here."

Zaheeb replied, "Well, you see, I actually surround this body. There is a part of me outside of this body and there is a part of me inside of this body. So, actually, I make this body move and do things for me, but it is just a vehicle or a means for me to do what I need it to do. When I am hurt, I speak to my body and it heals. We have a wonderful relationship with one another."

The visitor inquired, "You mean you actually do not live inside your body? Who are you then? What you are saying is very strange. I do not understand."

Zaheeb replied, "I am Me—you are looking at Me. It is just that my body is only a little part of Me. The way I can explain it is to ask you to look at that blade of grass. It has a green colour. When it dries, the green colour is gone. At different times of the day, when you look at it, the shade of the green colour is different. At night, there is no colour. So, I am like the blade of grass. The green colour is in it and is also ruled by what is around it—outside of it. When that green colour is gone, then what remains of the grass is brown and dry. It is like when this body can no longer be used by me, it will dry up like the grass—to a brown, lifeless colour. It is rather simple."

The visitor then said, "So you can heal your body whenever you wish?"

Zaheeb replied, "Yes, of course. I ask it to heal and it heals."

The older man then asked, "Do you ask it to heal in the same way as you ask the Sun for a ray to light your fire?"

Zaheeb smiled and said, "Yes—of course! Now you understand. It is very simple."

The older man then asked Zaheeb, "Who taught you to do these things?"

"You do not need to be taught about this," Zaheeb replied. "You just know it. I mean, when a baby is ready to walk, it just walks. No one needs to teach it to walk."

The visitor was amazed with what he was hearing. He then asked Zaheeb, "Can just anyone split the thunderclouds or draw the Sun's rays or heal his or her body?"

Zaheeb replied, "Well, I told you—all babies learn to walk. If you asked the baby about walking while it is lying down before it has learned to walk, it may not know what you are talking about. The baby would wonder how these two little things that it kicks about in the air can actually make it walk. But then, one day, it starts to walk and it puts its legs to good use. That's how it is."

The older man looked around at the fields and then pointed to the watercourse near them and said, "Does this river ever dry up?"

"Of course not," Zaheeb replied. "I just draw it from those white peaks of the mountain."

The visitor had learned so much. Zaheeb invited him to spend the night in his hut. At the appropriate time, the fire was lit and it looked like almost everything Zaheeb needed was provided for. As they ate dinner, the older man asked Zaheeb, "It looks to me like you have everything you need or want."

Zaheeb replied, "No, I am careful to only draw what I need. I keep the 'wants' away, for that can shut all the doors for me."

The other man was confused. "I do not understand what you mean," he said.

Zaheeb replied, "Well, you see, I told you that I live around and within this body. The 'wants' arise within this body, which will just dry up one day like the blade of grass. Therefore the 'wants' are of no significance. If one is not careful about the 'wants', one can get pulled completely within one's body. Then one becomes like the baby who had learned to walk but lost one of its legs in the process. How could such a baby ever run again?"

As they lay down to sleep, Zaheeb asked the older man, "Surely you know about these things or else you could never have found me."

The other man looked into Zaheeb's eyes and said, "That is true. But, like the baby, I had lost one leg. . . ."

Received on November 30, 1996.

SEVENTEEN

THE ℒIGHTHOUSE:
A UNIQUE EXPERIENCE IN MEDITATION

The Voice of Inspiration says to the Herald: *"Write about the experience of Maya as she rose in her meditation towards the Light. Relate the Symbols that she encountered in her meditation, for there is much to be learned from them."*

It is midnight and Maya, a young Indian girl, is sitting in contemplation in a pitch-dark room in a villa. The villa is situated at the top of a cliff, facing the Mediterranean Ocean, on an island off the North African coast. In her meditation, she has reached the moment when the entire Earth has become still. There is no wind, no sound, not even a little ripple in the Ocean. She feels as if her Soul is no longer in her body. In a strange way she can see herself in the distance, sitting in a little boat, looking into the beautiful dark star-filled sky. She asks herself, Where am I? Why is everything so still? Why is everything so quiet? Why can I not see anything in this darkness save for the beautiful, distant stars in the sky? She looks around herself and wonders why the air is neither hot nor cold. She asks herself, What kind of a place is this?

As Maya continues to sit in meditation in utter silence and stillness, a beautiful experience begins to engulf her, from her body to her mind to her Spirit. She begins to feel very, very light. She feels herself leave the boat and start to float gently in the air. As she drifts away, she sees her little boat merge into the darkness. Now she is floating by herself and there is nothing to carry her in the air like the boat did in the water. As she looks into the sky, the tiny stars continue to twinkle.

A cool breeze begins to blow by her; it gives her a new sense of strength and power. She is free to go wherever she wants. But she wonders, Where is that? She asks herself, Do I have a home? Where do I belong? Why am I alone? What happened to all those beloved ones that were with me once upon a time? She tries hard to remember, but her mind has ceased to function.

In the distance she sees a dull, flickering light that flashes on and off at regular intervals. This light does not sit on the ground; it is high up and it looks almost as if it is standing on a mountain. She begins to slowly head towards this light, gliding gently in the cool breeze. As she looks below, she can see the thin pencil of light reflect off the surface of the still water. As she draws closer, she realizes that she is heading towards a Lighthouse. But there are no boats in the Ocean or along the shore. There is no sign of life anywhere. She asks herself, Why is this Lighthouse standing tall, flashing this sharp beam of light into the darkness? What is it doing here? Why am I here? These thoughts repeatedly flash through her mind.

Then she calls out in the darkness, "O Lighthouse, you have drawn me from far away through your flashing light. Had I not seen you, I would have been drifting at this moment in a different direction. Yet you have drawn me here. Tell me, why did you do this?"

The Lighthouse replies, *"I have been here for a long, long time. In fact, my presence here has become timeless. I flash my light every day and every night, with the hope that I can help guide the travellers in the Ocean towards the safety of the shore. But when the winds blow harshly and the waves come crashing against the rocks, I can rarely guide anyone. Most of the people who travel in the Ocean in the rough sea are so busy protecting themselves from the waves that they are seldom able to see my light. I can see them, but they cannot see me. I can call out to them, but they cannot hear me. I can caution them about what lies ahead, but they can take no heed. Many a time, I have watched with sorrow beautiful people drift away into the deeper and darker Ocean without knowing that they had come so close to the safe shore. My heart cries out for them. What good am I to the traveller if he or she cannot see me?"*

Maya looks at this beautiful Lighthouse as she drifts closer to it and says, "How is it possible that today you have been able to draw me to you—to safety?"

The Lighthouse replies, *"You see, O Beloved One, you are travelling in total stillness—there is no motion around you. There is no wind. There are no waves. Everything is quiet. In fact, the stillness is so great that you are able to leave your boat and drift freely into the air. It is because of this stillness that you could look out into the distance and notice my light. There was nothing out there to distract you. Therefore my light reached you with great ease and I have guided you to the safe shore, in peace."*

Maya stops drifting and slowly descends onto the ground, at the foot of this special Lighthouse. As she looks up into the sky she sees its light flashing in the darkness. She then says to the Lighthouse, "I thank you for guiding me to the safe shore. From here, I can travel in peace on land until I reach the destination I am travelling to."

The Lighthouse replies, *"O Beloved Maya, it is not me you must thank. You must thank yourself, for you created the stillness within and around you. You silenced the winds and the waves, to such a point that you could drift by yourself in the air. You were no longer at any risk in the Ocean, therefore you no longer need me. Maya, it is this silence and the stillness that has shown you so much. Here I am, grateful to have guided you to the shore. Beloved Maya, when I look at you, I see your eyes closed. Yet I know that you see me and you see everything around you. When you open your eyes you will remember the flashing light of the Lighthouse, which will always be there to guide you.*

"O Beloved Maya, I am the Lighthouse that resides within you. I am always with you and I seek to guide you at all times. You stand at my feet now—our feet are together! Your face locks into my light. I am flashing this guiding light in your forehead. Your eyes are closed, but you can clearly see me because your mind has become totally still. Now I do not need to flash any more, for I do not need to attract your attention. You have seen me and I have guided you. Now I will shine continuously within you. I will guide you at all times. But remember, when your thoughts create turmoil in your mind, the waves will rage again and you will see me no more. I will have to flash again and hope that when you are able to create stillness within you, you will be able to recognize me again."

The Lighthouse continues, *"Maya, you have now seen the guiding light that has been and will be with you all your life. When you awake and look around you, all you will remember is your wonderful encounter with the Lighthouse. You have risen in meditation to the level of stillness that has allowed you to recognize so much. Remember, Maya, the Lighthouse that you see before you is no ordinary Symbol. It represents a beautiful start for you in your search for the Light of the Origin. Follow this Light and seek to come close to It. Remember, stillness is essential. Silence your mind and your surroundings. Then you can drift to the greatest heights of Knowledge. Make peace with yourself, O Beloved Maya, for you can then become a Lighthouse to all those around you. . . ."*

Received on October 2, 1997.

EIGHTEEN

ℋaseem's ℰscape:
The Parable of the Hermit

There was once an old man who lived in a little log cabin in the midst of a tropical forest in Asia. His name was Kaseem. He lived all by himself and enjoyed the small and large gifts that Nature bestowed upon him each day. Every morning he would awaken early and watch the sun rise. At noon, he would sit under the shade of the trees and enjoy the simple meal that he had prepared for himself. Every afternoon he would rest in his cabin as the tropical rainstorm hit. This was the time of day that he enjoyed the most, because he loved the notion of having a dry shelter that protected him from the rainstorm.

One afternoon as he lay on his bed looking out of his window at the rain, he saw a pretty white Dove come and sit on the window ledge. This was very unusual for Kaseem because white Doves were never seen in his part of the forest, especially in the midst of a tropical rainstorm! The bird looked at Kaseem and said, *"Greetings, O Kaseem—it is wonderful to see you again!"*

The old man was quite puzzled with this whole experience. How could a white Dove which he had never seen before be sitting on this window ledge and speaking to him? Kaseem replied, "O beautiful Bird, I have never, ever seen you before! Who are you and what brings you to my humble abode?"

The Dove smiled and said, *"My dear Kaseem, I have known you for a long, long time. I have been with you ever since you can remember. It is just that you have never cared to see me."*

The poor old man was now even more puzzled! He said to the Dove, "My dear bird, I have never set my eyes upon you before this day. What brings you here today?"

The Dove replied, *"I have come to teach you something that you desperately need to learn."*

"And what may that be?" Kaseem asked.

The Dove smiled and replied, *"Kaseem, why is it that you live here all by yourself, with no friends or companions?"*

The old man answered, "Well, I am quite happy to be here by myself."

The Dove looked into Kaseem's eyes and said, *"You know that is not true! You came to live here in the forest some fifteen years ago. You left a beautiful home in the town to come to this lonely place. Need I say any more?"*

The old man, certain now that this Bird was no ordinary creature, replied, "Yes, my dear Bird, you are correct. I experienced great turmoil in my life when I lived in my mansion in the town. I had arguments with my wife Saleema each day and my businesses made me miserable! I could not take the pressure. Then, when Saleema left me and took our son Shabeer with her, I decided I could no longer carry on with my life of misery. So I left the house and wandered with no direction into this forest. I built my home here and learned to enjoy the peace and quiet. I do not need any people around me to cause me pain! I do not need creditors chasing me to pay them their dues. I do not need to deal with the arguments with Saleema, and watch little Shabeer cry when we fight. That life was not for me. I have left it behind once and for all. Now I am happy to just live here amidst the trees."

The Dove looked sad and said, *"Kaseem, are you really happy? Did you not just run away from your problems? Did you not abandon your family, friends and loved ones just to escape from your own weakness?"*

Kaseem was very upset to hear this. He yelled at the Dove and said, "What do you know about pain? What do you know about how difficult my life was? What do you know about how lonely I felt when I first came here? What do you know about how I feel today? I have built a new life for myself here and that's what matters!"

The Dove quietly replied, *"Kaseem, you are not happy here. You ran away from life. What you have found here is a refuge that is so temporary. Your problems have not gone away. They are still very much alive in you. Why don't you try to resolve the conflicts that you carry within yourself? It is not too late, you know."*

Kaseem, very upset by now, replied, "Are you suggesting that I go back to that rat race and fight all those ugly battles again? You are one cruel bird! Why did you come here, anyway?"

The Dove replied, *"Kaseem, I have been with you for longer than you can or will remember. You carry turmoil within yourself. Running away from life is not the path of the courageous. Facing and dealing with obstacles is the path of strength. As you overcome each obstacle, you become stronger. It is like when the blacksmith works with his steel. The more he works it, the better and stronger it gets. By running away, you did not allow yourself to grow and strengthen. You took the path of the weak and remained weak. Go back, Kaseem, to your wife and your son. Face your beloved ones to whom you owe so much. Square your books with all those to whom you are obligated. Then if you leave you will find true peace wherever you go. In a funny way, you will never need to go anywhere because you will be at peace with yourself wherever you are."*

Kaseem knew that what the Dove was saying was very true. He was terribly unhappy from within and these fifteen years in isolation had not healed any of his pain. He then said, "My dear white Bird, you are full of wisdom. I know that what you say is true but I have no courage to go through all my pains again. At least here I am sheltered from them."

The Dove replied, *"Are you really sheltered from pain here? You carry this pain with you no matter where you go! Let me show you how to overcome your pain."*

Kaseem was delighted to find a solution. He anxiously said to the Dove, "I am ready; show me how."

The Dove smiled at Kaseem and said, *"Tell me why you love lying in this cabin every afternoon."*

Kaseem looked down in embarrassment and replied, "I love being in the shelter when the rain is pouring down outside."

The Dove replied, *"Precisely—you are hiding in here from the rain! You are afraid of the rain!"*

Kaseem objected, "I am not afraid of the rain! I do not like to get wet, that's all!"

The Dove then beckoned, *"Come out with me into the rain."*

With that, Kaseem stepped out of his cabin and stood in his yard, where the rain poured heavily over his head. He was immediately drenched! He looked at the Dove with disbelief. He was actually standing in the pouring rain, which was something he absolutely dreaded!

The Dove then commanded, *"Hold out your hands into the rain and dance around in circles. Feel free and dance!"*

Kaseem obeyed. He began to turn round and round with his open palms taking in the rain. He was completely soaked from head to foot! Just then, he began to feel a strange sense of happiness. He began to laugh as he spun around in the rain. Then he began to run and sing. It felt wonderful! He had not felt this way in all his fifteen years of self-exile in the forest! Kaseem was filled with joy. The rain made him feel happier than ever. Embracing the rain gave him power over what he so very much loathed!

He looked up at the sky and saw the Dove. It was no longer small. Its wings were as large as the sky itself!

The Dove looked down at Kaseem and said, *"You feel free, don't you? You embraced the rain which you hated so much and stayed away from for each and every day over the last fifteen years. Now you have found freedom and it makes you happy. It makes you feel powerful. You see, dear Kaseem, that's what you should have done fifteen years ago, before running away from your troubles. Embrace your troubles and you will gain power over them. Never run away from your problems, for they will follow you wherever you go! Thank the blessed rain that has set you free today. Go back home, for you have fifteen years of your life to catch up with."*

Kaseem knelt down and raised his arms into the sky as he addressed the Dove. "You are truly a blessed Bird. You have taught me so much in such a short time. I will go back home today and pick up my life from where I left. What a wonderful sight it will be to see my dear son Shabeer again. I wonder if Saleema will forgive me? What if she doesn't?"

The Dove exclaimed, *"There you go, fearing again! If she does not forgive you, try again and again until she does. Remember how the rain that you loathed set you free? Go in haste, for your loved ones are awaiting you, Kaseem!"*

The old man looked at the Dove, which had grown even larger than the sky itself. He inquired, "How can you tell that they are waiting for me?"

The Dove replied, *"I see what they see, hear what they hear and feel what they feel. You have left a deep void in their lives through your sudden departure. Your poor loved ones look at the stars each night wondering whether you are alive and well and looking at the same stars. In their lowest moments, they fear that you are dead and gone. This terrible void and hurt that you have inflicted upon them must be healed. No one but you can do this."*

The Dove continued, *"Every man, woman and child in this world is granted a precise and fixed amount of time to fulfil their life's purpose before embarking upon their Ultimate Journey. Kaseem, I came here to open up your eyes to the important things that you need to do before it is time to take your Ultimate Journey."*

Kaseem understood what the Dove was trying to tell him. "My time in this world is over, isn't it?" he asked.

The Dove replied, *"Yes, Kaseem, it is time for you to leave. Go back and make your amends. I will see you again in six days and five nights. You will then join me on a beautiful Journey."*

Kaseem then gratefully said, "I thank you for blessing me with the six days and five nights. I will complete what I have to complete and then be ready to embrace my death."

The Dove smiled and asked, *"Aren't you afraid of death now, Kaseem? Aren't you afraid of joining me on the Ultimate Journey?"*

Kaseem smiled back and replied, "I am not afraid of anything any more. Besides, I would love to join you and sing and dance in a thousand rain clouds! I would not give that up for anything, O dear Bird."

The Dove began to flap its wings and fly away. Kaseem then heard the beautiful voice from the sky call out, *"So be it, Kaseem."*

Received on February 7, 1998.

(Continued in Chapter 19)

NINETEEN

Kaseem's Escape: the Journey Home

(Continued from Chapter 18)

As Kaseem watched the Dove disappear over the horizon, he realized that he had a lot left to accomplish in the six nights and five days that the Dove had given him. Without further delay, he set out on his journey back to the town he had left fifteen years ago. He walked throughout the day and the night, taking only short breaks to rest. At his age, he tired easily, but he was not willing to lose the precious little time that he had left.

At last, as the forest came to en end, he could see the town ahead of him. His heart beat rapidly with excitement. As he entered the town, he looked around, bewildered at how much had changed over the fifteen years. The green fields were now little concrete jungles. There were many new faces that he had never seen before. In fact, he could not recognize anybody! Poor Kaseem felt like a complete stranger!

Finally, as he spotted his villa, he felt relieved to notice the familiar old trees and the quaint little park that lay in front of it. He was home! He hid for a moment behind the tall old tree that stood next to the verandah. His heart leapt with joy as he saw Saleema, sitting on their favourite bench in the verandah, knitting. She had aged. Her hair had turned grey but she still looked as beautiful to Kaseem as the day he had married her! He felt a strong urge to run over and embrace her. He had missed her dearly over his fifteen-year self-exile. As he watched her, he began to feel afraid. What if she didn't want to see him? How was he going to handle her rejection? As his mind raced with a thousand thoughts, he heard the voice of the Dove remind him, *"Embrace that which you fear and you will have power over it."*

Just as Kaseem was about to step forward, the front door of the villa swung open. A handsome young man, six feet tall and dark, stepped out. It was Shabeer! Kaseem felt a lump in his throat. He broke down and started to cry. How could he ever have left behind the two most important people in his life, and for such a long time? When he last saw Shabeer his son was only a child. And now, standing at the door, was a young man!

Shabeer heard the sound of Kaseem's sobs. He quickly ran over to the tree to see what was wrong. Suddenly he found himself standing in front of this poor old man, who was weeping profusely by now. "Dad," cried Shabeer, "is it you?"

Kaseem looked up at his son, unsure of what he should do. Shabeer hugged his father. In a tearful voice he asked, "Where have you been for so long?" Poor Kaseem had no words to say. It felt so good to hold his beloved son.

Meanwhile, Saleema had heard all this noise and walked over to the tree to see what was going on. Her heart stopped when she saw her son hugging an old man! It was Kaseem, her long-lost husband! She ran over, wailing, "Kaseem, you are back! You are back!" The three were united in a tearful reunion.

Kaseem was overwhelmed with the outpouring of affection from his loved ones. All these years, he had feared their rejection. He had come back prepared to face his worst fears and instead, here he was being received with such great warmth! He remembered the words of the Dove, *"Embrace that which you fear and you will have power over it."* How true, Kaseem thought to himself!

The next day Kaseem set about trying to settle all his outstanding obligations. Over the years, Shabeer had built a successful little business and he now helped his father in every way he could to settle their debts. The people who once knew and hated Kaseem were astonished at his return. They were even more astonished with the humility that he showed as he sought their forgiveness. Where has all the ego and arrogance gone? they wondered. Their memories of Kaseem had been most unpleasant, to say the least! And now here they were, faced by a humble, loving old man, who had come to make his amends.

Kaseem was forgiven. He was even accepted back into his little world as a new man, someone who, in a strange way, had found a special place in people's hearts—even the ones that he had loathed all these years!

On the sixth night, he sat with Shabeer and Saleema and told them about his encounter with the Dove. He also told them that the time had come for him to leave this world. Poor Shabeer and Saleema were heartbroken!

"My beloved Kaseem," Saleema said, "after losing you for fifteen years, it was so wonderful to have found you again. What a special man you have become! Although I cannot bear the thought of losing you again, I am so grateful for the beautiful memory that Shabeer and I will have of you now. Before you returned, each time we thought of you, we felt sad and afraid. We wondered whether you were alive or dead! Each time we talked about you, all we felt was pain. Now when you leave we will remember these special days and wonderful moments. Kaseem, we will celebrate your life! You will live in our hearts and Souls forever."

Kaseem shuddered at the thought of having died in the forest without having seen his beloved ones. What kind of a memory would he have left them with? What kind of a legacy would he have left with the people of the town? He quietly thanked the Dove for giving him the chance to correct his wrongs. His fifteen years in the forest now felt like fifteen minutes!

"O my beloved ones," he now said to his wife and son, "I will leave you this time in peace. I have learned so much from you. I have learned how it feels to be forgiven, when I never knew how to forgive. I have learned how it feels to be loved, when I never knew how to love. I do not know the Journey that lies ahead of me, but I have embraced it with joy. One thing that life has taught me is to embrace my fears with open arms. When I ran away from my fear, it had power over me—for fifteen long years. No sooner did I embrace my fear, it was gone!"

Kaseem continued, "After seeing you both again and spending these precious last few days with you, I have also learned that we are all given a second chance in our lives to correct our mistakes. This is indeed a special blessing. After each terrible experience comes a time and a chance to make our amends. I came back to you not knowing what to expect. I came prepared to be rejected by everyone and instead I found so much love. Even if you had all rejected me, I would still have been grateful for having taken my second chance!"

Kaseem could see the beautiful Dove in the distance, flying towards him. He said to Saleema and Shabeer, "My friend the Dove is here to take me on a beautiful Journey of discovery. My life in this world has taught me much and I will take this knowledge with me on this next great Journey."

Kaseem passed away peacefully. Saleema joined him a few years later. Shabeer grew to become one of the most successful businessmen in the country. He shared the story of Kaseem and the Dove with people all over the world. He lived his life without fear. He stood firm in the face of all his problems and adversities, for he had learned to embrace them wholeheartedly.

One day as the Dove looked down on Shabeer, it smiled and said to Kaseem and Saleema, *"He doesn't need me any more...."*

Received on January 18, 1999.

TWENTY

𝒾nfluencing 𝒯omorrow:
The Message of Self Empowerment

The Voice of Inspiration says to the Herald: *"The world is going through a major change. When you look at how people react today towards global events, you would be most surprised! Fifty years ago, the consciousness that humanity has today would have been viewed as ridiculous! How often do people stop to ask the question, 'Why is this happening?' Clearly the answer lies in the fact that the Earth is undergoing a significant transformation.*

"In physical terms, this can be seen in changes in weather patterns, vegetation, natural events and lots more. In spiritual terms, there is an awakening in all Creation which will

cause progress in a very positive direction. Harmony is the ultimate goal of this entire transformation process.

"Will it indeed be achieved? The answer lies in the hands of humanity. In the past thousands of years, the world often approached this Harmony, but then the actions of humanity distorted the process, resulting in a serious reversal! This was often followed by destruction of an untold magnitude! Hence when people read what is set forth in this Chapter, they should pause and reflect. This very special process of leading towards Harmony has indeed begun and is gaining rapid pace everywhere.

"Look at how the world reacted towards the death of the beautiful Princess Diana! What do you think caused such an outpouring of love? What you witnessed was a demonstration of the inner awakening that is occurring within people. This is why they are reacting the way they do! Diana's passing from her physical form was a process that had to be. It was ordained that way. However, the impact of her death revealed a unique awakening in people throughout the world. Therefore, what is most important is that humanity should ride over the crests of the beautiful waves that will lead to a change of a very (special) substantial magnitude.

Influencing Tomorrow: the Message of Self Empowerment

"The future of this civilization is indeed very bright. However, it must be remembered that this special process can be disrupted by humanity and, in particular, by the actions and directions that will be taken by the Superpowers of today. There is a polarization of power in two parts of the world. In the West there is the United States of America, trailed closely by Europe, and in the East there is China. The actions and interactions of each of these Superpowers will have a direct influence on the process of transformation that is currently occurring.

"When you look back in history, the process of transformation was disrupted time and time again by the actions of polarized power bases in civilizations. Today it is no different, except for one unique aspect which can make all the difference. You see, historically, Superpowers led the direction of the world; all other nations and peoples were powerless bystanders. Today, this is not so.

"The power of communication has yielded the potential for unity within humanity like never before. Hence the people of the world today can influence the direction that will be taken by the Superpowers. The awakening in each being is very strong and there is a natural Empowerment that is being carried within each and every person today. For that matter, this Empowerment

rests in each and every element of Nature. This has never been the case before.

"However, whilst this Unity and Empowerment give hope that the positive changes will prevail, there is also a very real threat that needs to be overcome. This threat will be greater from the East than from the West. There will indeed be clashes between the Superpowers in the coming years. These clashes will be ones of ideology, values, economics, politics and military power. These differences and clashes could have devastating consequences on the process of Harmony. How can humanity ensure that this does not happen? There are some very clear answers to this question, which if followed correctly could in fact harness the strengths of the Superpowers to the benefit of humanity at large.

"The first and most important step is to build upon and strengthen the Empowerment that exists in each and every being today. This can be done through various steps. To start with, people need to go back and take a hard look at their faith—not from the perspective of rituals, but rather from the viewpoint of its Essence. They should try to identify and recognize with clarity the values, ethics and Essence of their faith, and put these important elements into action each and every moment of their lives. This will build Empowerment. For those who do

not have a faith, or believe in anything, it would help them to take a look at the Statement of Universal Truth, which says, 'I am You, You are Me and Together We are Everything.' They may glean whatever meaning they can from this wonderful Statement, and put it into practice. Most importantly, people should try to focus their attention towards the non-material aspects of their lives. There must be a blend and balance between the purely material and the spiritual. This will strengthen the Empowerment.

"Second, the world must learn to resolve conflict by reasoning rather than war. The reasoning must be driven by ethics and the spiritual balance, which in itself is inherently non-confrontational. As humanity begins to create this approach, the impact will be clearly imprinted within the decision-making process of the Superpowers. It is important to recognize and understand that none of the Superpowers are bad or evil. The mere polarization of power is the problem. This polarization can bring strength or it can lead to supreme chaos! Hence the correct harnessing of the energies of the Superpowers is indeed essential.

"In this regard, the movement towards political and economic depolarization between nations is very important. The formation of regional economies and liberalization of the flow of people within these regions and

between nations will serve to create stronger unity and hence, Harmony. This approach will clearly neutralize the impact of any disruptions that will be caused through differences between the Superpowers. As a matter of fact, this approach will thin down the Superpowers in themselves. This depolarization will come about as people exercise their will to unite with their neighbours—from family to family, street to street, town to town, city to city, nation to nation and continent to continent.

The next solution, which is also very important, is for the people of the world to unite in ensuring that practices of oppression between races, genders, nations and religions be peacefully discouraged. There are places in the world where freedom to practise one's faith is not allowed. There are places in the world where a great deal of injustice prevails against women, who were indeed created as equals to men. Then there are places where political ideologies are imposed upon people against their will. All these kinds of practices need to be peacefully discouraged. This can be achieved if people live within the bond of unity, governed by ethics of fairness, mutual respect and love. As the oppressors find themselves surrounded by neighbours who live their lives in a positive, exemplary fashion, they will have no choice but to change. Nations need to elect leaders who have the humility, consciousness and desire to promote and achieve such peaceful changes.

"The best example of how to set about accomplishing this important process is to look at a gardener who is trying to change the direction of the stem of one of his indoor plants. If he bends it with his hands, he will break the stem and kill the plant. So what can he do? He can alter the position or direction of the sunlight towards where he would like the stem to turn. In time, he will accomplish this desired change. The stem will have bent, freely and happily. But remember that this process takes longer than the quick approach of physically bending the stem. Therefore, patience is important. If people change in the right direction, so will their neighbours, in time.

"Humanity draws most of its strength from its environment. Hence as people learn to love and respect their surroundings, and as pollution and environmentally destructive practices are relegated to the past, the strength of the Empowerment will grow. Humanity may then be able to ride the crests of the waves of progress.

"In the coming years, the world will witness some very powerful events, ranging from severe natural catastrophes to positive scientific discoveries that will shape the course of the future. Whilst natural catastrophes will be

experienced in North America, of proportions never experienced in this part of the world to date, the greater toll will be taken within Asia. Humanity has the power today to avert these natural disasters by building upon its Empowerment. This Chapter has only revealed a few of numerous ways to achieve this strength. Through special inner inspirations, people will find more and more ways to achieve Empowerment. This will often require them to make significant changes in their attitudes and lifestyles. This should not be too difficult because whatever changes they choose to make in this regard may lead them in a more positive direction.

"In conclusion, here is an important thought to reflect upon: There is a day in the not too distant future, when people will wake up in the midst of massive conflict and war. This conflict will have been born from the River that is Red. Everywhere in the world there will be anxiety and fear. A big process of change will have occurred that will have disrupted the beautiful process of transformation of the Earth towards Harmony. All that has been achieved by humanity will be reversed. The lengths of the days and nights will have changed—and lots more. This day has been experienced by the world before in its history, and the cycle is simply repeating itself. Yet this dreadful day can

be completely averted by humanity forever, if people begin to heed the advice that has been given in this Chapter. Never before in history has every human being possessed so much inner power to change the future of this planet for the better. Never before in history have such tools of instantaneous global communication been available to humanity as there are today. Therefore, now is the perfect time for people of all nations, races and cultures to unite and build upon this special Empowerment, which is truly a blessing indeed!

Received on September 26, 1997.

$\mathcal{Q}$uotes for $\mathcal{R}$eflection

The forest has taught me that everyone and everything is equal. All creation is equal. None is above another. You are the king, but above you is a Greater King.

The Power of Love: The Parable of Ariana & Swaleem, Chapter 1, page 9.

No riches of any kingdom could measure up against the treasure of their love.

The Power of Love: The Parable of Ariana & Swaleem, Chapter 1, page 12.

There are things in our lives that are so precious. We never stop to recognize them, for we are too busy being the centres of our little universes.

The Power of Love: The Parable of Ariana & Swaleem, Chapter 1, page 15.

Life is a multitude of Experiences. There are things we can control and then there are things we cannot control. The amount of commitment and effort that we put into our businesses, professions, relationships and all other activities clearly rests in our hands. However, we cannot control the outcome of our efforts. Success or failure is not in our hands.

The Saint in Central Park: The Parable of the Chief Executive, Chapter 2, page 18.

If you make life a contest between success and defeat, you will feel highs and suffer lows.

The Saint in Central Park: The Parable of the Chief Executive, Chapter 2, page 19.

You must live each day as if it were your last. Then ask yourself how you feel about worldly success or failure.

The Saint in Central Park: The Parable of the Chief Executive, Chapter 2, page 19.

You have always taken tomorrow for granted; you have automatically assumed that it would be there. This is where you often go wrong. You should aim to start each day by assuming that there will be no tomorrow. Now make today's decisions accordingly.

The Saint in Central Park: The Parable of the Chief Executive, Chapter 2, page 20.

One of the most important purposes of human life is to seek Knowledge and gain Experience. Success or failure are less important than the Experience that is gained from every situation.

Making Wise Decisions: The Parable of the Gold Trader, Chapter 3, page 24.

In life, nothing is clearly black or white. Everything exists in shades of grey and this is why human beings have been blessed with the Intellect to make decisions within this intricate context.

Making Wise Decisions: The Parable of the Gold Trader, Chapter 3, page 24.

In every human being I see a Soul, which I believe comes from a very pure Origin. I believe that all Souls start from the "good." Hence, each being has a fundamental Essence which is "good." But the Mind, which is detached from the Essence, is where greed and treachery exist.

Making Wise Decisions: The Parable of the Gold Trader, Chapter 3, page 30.

I believe that every relationship must be based on a "Bond of Trust." This bond comes from wisdom and Experience, which help us select the relationships we want to keep and how we want to manage them.

Making Wise Decisions: The Parable of the Gold Trader, Chapter 3, page 32.

The most complex of problems that people face can be solved by the simplest of things.

The Alps: A Symbol of Humility,
Chapter 4, page 35.

As mountains become taller, their snow covers become larger and denser. Therefore, when people rise higher in whatever they do, they should become more humble, like the mountains.

The Alps: A Symbol of Humility,
Chapter 4, page 37.

Fear comes from one's inability to embrace the unknown. Fear stems from lack of Faith. Faith adds a dimension of "knowing" to the "unknown." At the Dawn of Life, at birth, one starts with 100 percent of the unknown that lies ahead of oneself. At the Dusk of Life, at death, one leaves with 100 percent knowledge, for there are no unknowns.

Fear: The Parable of the Slave,
Chapter 5, page 39.

At every point in your life, you have a choice that you can make. It is only after you have made this choice that circumstances take over.

Detachment: The Parable of the Swiss Merchant,
Chapter 6, page 54.

All your life you have been obsessed by your ambitions and your material well-being. During this period some wonderful moments of love, affection and warmth have passed you by, without your being aware if it.

Detachment: The Parable of the Swiss Merchant,
Chapter 6, page 55.

If you Detach yourself from your business and material activities for a certain amount of time each day, you will begin to discover and become Attached to your loved ones. In this, you will find much happiness.

Detachment: The Parable of the Swiss Merchant,
Chapter 6, page 55.

Detachment brings freedom. This freedom allows you to flow like water towards whatever it is that you desire.

Detachment: The Parable of the Swiss Merchant, Chapter 6, page 56.

I cannot tell you how many cycles you have left, but I can say that some of them will be long, dark and painful, while others will be joyous and fulfilling. Such is the beauty of your journey.

The Raindrop and the Blade of Grass: A Parable of Life Cycles, Chapter 7, page 62.

In the plane of the Eternal exist Souls who are governed by neither time nor space. They exist purely within a simple State of Being.

The Message of Reincarnation: The Parable of Tara, Chapter 8, page 64.

When one commits suicide, one's Soul dwells in a state of "no belonging." It no longer has a physical form to give it material expression. It does not belong within the Eternal State, either, It is wandering and lost.

The Message of Reincarnation: The Parable of Tara, Chapter 8, page 70.

A mountain stands tall and strong and there is much to be learned by looking at its sides. The events in a person's life are very comparable to the stories that are written along the sides of a mountain. There is much to be learned from them.

Kilimanjaro: A Parable of Life's Perspectives, Chapter 9, page 73.

The humans are a race that loves to be played with, and the mountain has its fun by placing illusions all around them!

Kilimanjaro: A Parable of Life's Perspectives, Chapter 9, page 77.

I suppose a person's life is like the slope of the mountain, full of surprises and appearances that change every moment without warning!

Kilimanjaro: A Parable of Life's Perspectives, Chapter 9, page 79.

Every observation carries a unique combination of perspectives. Each perspective is always correct for its beholder. Most conflicts arise from intolerance towards other people's perspectives. Most successes are achieved through attitudes of confidence that have been regulated by wisdom that comes from being able to identify the potholes along the road.

Kilimanjaro: A Parable of Life's Perspectives, Chapter 9, page 80.

In today's age, people enjoy freedom of expression. They are free to exercise the broadest horizons of their Intellect. They cannot accept blindly the practice of a faith which is clouded with fear, restrictions, divisions and excessive material demands.

The Ancient Church Bell: A Message from the Great Soul, Chapter 10, page 86.

Building fences is the worst thing one can ever do. The moment we build a fence, we begin to shrink from outside and from within. The more fences we build, the quicker we will disappear. When God created this Earth, it had no boundaries. Human beings built fences which formed countries. As a civilization, we have continued to shrink from within throughout this cycle. We started as one family and now we have become hundreds of countries.

Fences: The Parable of the Thai Farmer, Chapter 11, page 92.

Giving is an essence of Nature. Inscribe in the hearts of your children the Law of the Eternal Pool. Inscribe in their hearts that each time they give, no matter how little or how much, they are keeping the Flow of the Eternal Pool going. If they were to receive ten fruits, they should give back at least one fruit, for the Flow must always prevail.

The Eternal Pool: The Parable of Ibrahim and Sarah, Chapter 12, page 98.

He or she who has true Authority never needs to exercise it, for the Will of the other always follows. Authority and Will are like two poles of a magnet—they must attract! The introduction of Fear destroys this harmony.

The Bedouin: A Parable of the Desert, Chapter 14, page 116.

As he watched the globe spinning steadily, Rahim realized that all the phases of life were clearly represented here. The purity, peace and beauty of the North Pole marked the start of life. The Equator marked its peak and the South Pole marked its end.

The Spinning Globe: A Parable of the Cycle of Life, Chapter 15, page 124.

The Sun is not hot. The Sun is like a tree that grows a hundred different types of fruit. Whatever fruit you seek, it will give to you.

Drawing Upon the Powers of Nature: The Parable of the Himalayan Shepherd, Chapter 16, page 133.

Stillness is essential. Silence your mind and your surroundings. Then you can drift to the greatest heights of Knowledge.

The Lighthouse: A Unique Experience in Meditation, Chapter 17, page 144.

Embrace your troubles and you will gain power over them. Never run away from your problems, for they will follow you wherever you go!

Kaseem's Escape: The Parable of the Hermit, Chapter 18, page 151.

Embrace that which you fear and you will have power over it.

Kaseem's Escape: The Journey Home, Chapter 19, page 155.

I have learned how it feels to be forgiven, when I never knew how to forgive.

Kaseem's Escape: The Journey Home, Chapter 19, page 158.

I have learned how it feels to be loved, when I never knew how to love.

Kaseem's Escape: The Journey Home, Chapter 19, page 158.

We are all given a second chance in our lives to correct our mistakes. This is indeed a special blessing.

Kaseem's Escape: The Journey Home, Chapter 19, page 159.

The world must learn to resolve conflict by reasoning rather than war. The reasoning must be driven by ethics and the spiritual balance, which in itself is inherently non-confrontational.

Influencing Tomorrow: The Message of Self Empowerment, Chapter 20, page 165.

The movement towards political and economic depolarization between nations is very important. The formation of regional economies and liberalization of the flow of people within these regions and between nations will serve to create stronger unity and hence, Harmony.

Influencing Tomorrow: The Message of Self Empowerment, Chapter 20, page 165.

In the coming years, the world will witness some very powerful events, ranging from severe natural catastrophes to positive scientific discoveries that will shape the course of the future.

Influencing Tomorrow: The Message of Self Empowerment, Chapter 20, page 167.

Never before in history has every human being possessed so much inner power to change the future of this planet for the better.

Influencing Tomorrow: The Message of Self Empowerment, Chapter 20, page 169.

About the Author

After escaping a near-fatal motorcycle accident in Kashmir in 1986, Amyn Dahya underwent a major transformation. He suddenly became a more peaceful man and he began to understand Creation like never before. Seven years later, in 1993, he was caught unaware as he repeatedly received inspirations so powerful that he was compelled to share them with the world.

Born in East Africa and educated in the United Kingdom, Amyn Dahya is a Professional Engineer and international businessman involved with the provision of safe drinking-water supply to disease-stricken areas. He is also actively involved with developing and promoting technologies to protect and cleanse the environment and remediate damage caused by industrial pollution and toxic spills.

When his first book, *Reflections from the Origin*, came out in 1998, Amyn Dahya said, "The writing of this book has been one of the greatest learning experiences of my life. I have been granted Knowledge from the Origin, which I am honoured to share with my fellow beings."

With the release of *Parables from the Origin*, Amyn Dahya continues, "These books will strike chords in the hearts and Souls of people of all races, cultures and religions. After all, they were written for them."

REFLECTIONS PUBLISHING
3908 Creekside Place, Burnaby, B.C. V5G 2P9
Phone: 604 926 4764
email: reflect@compuserve.com

Invoice # ....
Invoice Date ....

Invoice to / Ordered by: **Ship to:**

....
....
....
....

Contact: ....   Contact: ....
Daytime Phone: ....   Daytime Phone: ....

QUANTITY	DESCRIPTION	UNIT PRICE	AMOUNT
	Reflections from the Origin		
	Parables from the Origin		

SUBTOTAL	$
APPLICABLE TAXES	$
	$
SHIPPING & HANDLING	$
TOTAL	$

SPECIAL VOLUME DISCOUNTS
1 to 5 copies — 10%
6 to 10 — 15%
11 to 20 — 20%
Over 20 — 25%

CANADA
Reflections @ $19.95
Parables @ $12.95
add 7% GST
Shipping @ $6.00 for initial book,
$5.00 each additional book

USA
Reflections @ $17.95
Parables @ $9.95
Shipping @ $5.00 for initial book,
$3.50 each additional book

INTERNATIONAL
Please use US$ rates
Shipping @ $6.50 per book

PAYMENT METHOD

☐ VISA ☐ MasterCard ☐ American Express
☐ Cheque (payable to *Reflections Publishing*)

Name..
Card No. ....
Expiry Date ....
Signature..

If this is a gift and you wish to include a message, we will be happy to do so for you.

THANK YOU FOR YOUR ORDER.